Shri Lalitha Sahasranama Stotram

The One Thousand Names of Devi

RUPA

Published in Sanskriti Press
by Rupa Publications India Pvt. Ltd 2025
7/16, Ansari Road, Daryaganj
New Delhi 110002

Sales centres:
Bengaluru Chennai
Hyderabad Jaipur Kathmandu
Kolkata Mumbai Prayagraj

ISBN: 978-93-6156-157-3

First impression 2025

10 9 8 7 6 5 4 3 2 1

Printed in India

Introduction

At Sanskriti Press, we are deeply committed to preserving and sharing the rich landscape of India's spiritual and religious heritage. Our endeavor is to bring timeless texts to readers, fostering a connection with the profound wisdom of ancient traditions. It is with this vision that we present the *Lalitha Sahasranama*, a revered scripture that enumerates the thousand sacred names of the Divine Mother, Goddess Lalita.

The *Lalitha Sahasranama* is a celebrated Hindu text, particularly within Shaktism, the tradition devoted to the worship of Shakti, the Divine Feminine. This exquisite scripture, written in Sanskrit, is part of the *Brahmanda Purana*, an ancient text that delves into the mysteries of cosmic creation and the divine order of the universe. The thousand names within this text encapsulate the goddess's manifold attributes, accomplishments, and symbolism. These names are not merely descriptive but are chanted or sung as mantras, resonating deeply with spiritual seekers.

Lalitha Devi, also known as Tripura Sundari, embodies the supreme manifestation of feminine energy. She is revered as the consort of Lord Shiva and hailed as the epitome of beauty, grace, power, and compassion. Representing the divine cycle of creation, sustenance, and dissolution, she is the wellspring of existence itself.

The very name *Lalitha* translates to "She who plays," signifying her spontaneous and joyous nature. Her thousand names, poetically woven with occasional wordplay, are presented in the form of hymns (*stotras*) or broken into individual mantras (*namavali*). Uniquely, the *Lalitha Sahasranama* features exactly 1000 names without repetition, avoiding auxiliary conjunctions often used in similar texts. This meticulous composition meets the highest metrical, poetic, and mystic standards, enhancing its sacredness.

Legend has it that the *Lalitha Sahasranama* was composed by the eight *vaag devis*—Vasini, Kameshvari, Aruna, Vimala, Jayani, Modini, Sarveshvari, and Kaulini—at the command of Goddess Lalita herself. The text is introduced within the *Brahmanda Purana* through a divine discourse between Hayagriva, an incarnation of Lord Vishnu, and the sage Agastya. This sacred hymn is said to have been revealed in the temple of Thirumeyachur near Kumbakonam or alternatively at the Upanishad Bramham Mutt in Kanchipuram.

The *Lalitha Sahasranama* invites devotees to immerse themselves in the Divine Mother's grace, as she bestows her blessings upon those whom she chooses to worship her. We hope that this edition, brought to you by Sanskriti Press, helps deepen your spiritual journey and enrich your connection with the timeless wisdom of the Divine Feminine.

Lalitha Sahasranama

The thousand names of Sri Lalitha forms a part of the Brahmanda Purana as a conversation between Hayagriva and sage Agasthya, who probably introduced it to the worshippers of Southern India. According to the legends, it was originally composed by the eight goddesses of speech (vagdevis), directly under the supervision of the goddess herself and conveyed to the world through Hayagriva and Vyasa. It is an encomium to the Goddess Lalitha Thripura Sundari, extolling her virtues, victories, associations, aspects, greatness, perfections, powers, and manifestations. The Sahasranama has a great significance in Hinduism because it is used in the ritual and spiritual worship of most goddesses, such as Parvathi, Durga, Kali, Lakshmi, Sarasvathi, Bhagavathi, etc. It is used in recitations (parayana), ritual worship (homas), meditation and contemplation (dhyana). It is unique for its structural composition, metrical beauty, and spiritual value in knowing and understanding the numerous powers and manifestations of Shakti.

Sri Lalitha is the Mother Goddess, an aspect of Durga, and consort of Kameswara (Shiva), who combines in herself both the immanent and transcendental powers. She resides in the divine city of Nagara, at the top of the Meru Mountain. Famously known as Maha Tripura Sundari, the beauty of the three cities, she is known for her extreme beauty and ferocity, with long and flowing hair, lotus like eyes, vigorous body, and extreme brilliance. She is not only feminine, homely, loving, and delicate but also extremely fierce, proud, intimidating, and courageous. She rules the hearts and minds of her devotees, gods and goddesses, spiritual teachers, students and common people. While she casts her bewitching spell on everyone, she readily destroys it when she is worshipped with devotion.

The Puranas state that she is easily pleased by worship, prayers, and devotion and quickly grants boons to her beloved devotees. She slew the demon Bandasura, leading a large army of Shiva ganas, Nitya Devathas, Avarna Devathas and great Shaktis like Chandini, Anima, Mahima, Brahmi, Kaumari, Jwalamalini, Bala, Vaishnavi, Varahi, Mahendri, Chamundi, Maha Lakshmi. She is also the resplendent goddess who is situated in all the Chakras as the great serpent power, Kundalini. The following prayer addressed to her elevates her both as the Supreme Goddess and Brahman himself in his numerous aspects as Brahma, Vishnu, and Shiva. The Lalitha Sahasranama Sthothram is a very auspicious prayer, containing the thousand names in 182 verses.

।। न्यासः ।।

अस्य श्री ललिता सहस्रनामस्तोत्र माला मन्त्रस्य ।
वशिन्यादिवाग्देवता ऋषयः ।
अनुष्टुप् छन्दः ।
श्रीललिता परमेश्वरी देवता ।
श्रीमद्वाग्भवकूटेति बीजम् ।
मध्यकूटेति शक्तिः । शक्तिकूटेति कीलकम् ।
श्रीललिता महा त्रिपुरसुन्दरी प्रसादसिद्धिद्वारा
चिन्तितफलावाप्त्यर्थे जपे विनियोगः ।।

Nyāsaḥ

Asya śrīlalitāsahasranāmastotramālā
mantrasya.
vaśinyādivāgdevatā ṛṣayaḥ.
anuṣṭup chandaḥ.
śrīlalitā parameśvarī devatā

śrīmadvāgbhavakūṭeti bījam
madhyakūṭeti śaktiḥ. śaktikūṭeti kīlakam.
śrīlalitā mahā tripurasundarī
prasādasiddhidvārā
cintitaphalāvāptyarthe jape viniyogaḥ

।। ध्यानम् ।।

सिन्दूरारुण विग्रहां त्रिनयनां माणिक्यमौलि स्फुरत्
तारा नायक शेखरां स्मितमुखी मापीन वक्षोरुहाम् ।
पाणिभ्यामलिपूर्ण रत्न चषकं रक्तोत्पलं बिभ्रतीं
सौम्यां रत्न घटस्थ रक्तचरणां ध्यायेत् परामम्बिकाम् ।।

Dhyānaṁ

Ōṁ sindūrāruna vigrahāṁ trinayanāṁ
mānikyamauli sphurat
tārā nāyaka śēkharāṁ smitamukhī
māpīna vakṣōruhāṁ
pānibhyāmalipūrna ratna caṣakaṁ
raktōtpalaṁ bibhratīṁ
saumyāṁ ratna ghatastha raktacaranāṁ
dhyāyēt parāmambikāṁ

May we meditate on the Divine Mother, whose body has the red hue of vermilion, who has three eyes, who wears a beautiful crown studded with rubies, who is adorned with the crescent Moon, whose face sports beautiful smile indicating compassion, who has beautiful limbs, whose hands hold a jewel-studded golden vessel filled with nectar, and in the other a red lotus flower.

अरुणां करुणातरङ्गिताक्षीं
धृतपाशाङ्कुशपुष्पबाणचापाम् ।
अणिमादिभिरावृतां मयुखैः
अहमित्येव विभावये भवानीम् ।।

aruṇāṁ karuṇā taraṅgitākṣīṁ
dhṛta pāśāṅkuśa puṣpa bāṇacāpām
aṇimādibhi rāvṛtāṁ mayūkhai-
rahamityeva vibhāvaye bhavānīm

I meditate on the great Empress. She is red in color, and her eyes are full of compassion, and holds the noose, the goad, the bow and the flowery arrow in Her hands. She is surrounded on all sides by powers such as aNimA for rays and She is the Self within me.

ध्यायेत्पद्मासनस्थां विकसितवदनां पद्मपत्रायताक्षीं
हेमाभां पीतवस्त्रां करकलितलसद्धेमपद्मां वराङ्गीम् ।
सर्वालङ्कारयुक्तां सततमभयदां भक्तनम्रां भवानीं
श्रीविद्यां शान्तमूर्तिं सकलसुरनुतां सर्वसम्पत्प्रदात्रीम् ।।

dhyāyet padmāsanasthāṁ
vikasitavadanāṁ padmapatrāyatākṣīṁ
hemābhāṁ pītavastrāṁ
karakalitalasaddhemapadmāṁ varāṅgīm
sarvālaṅkāra yuktāṁ satata mabhayadāṁ
bhaktanamrāṁ bhavānīṁ śrīvidyāṁ śānta
mūrtiṁ sakala suranutāṁ
sarva sampatpradātrīm

The Divine Goddess is to be meditated upon as seated on the lotus with petal eyes. She is golden hued, and has lotus flowers in Her hand. She dispels fear of the devotees who bow before Her. She is the embodiment of peace, knowledge (vidya), is praised by gods and grants every kind of wealth wished for.

सकुङ्कुमविलेपनामलिकचुम्बिकस्तूरिकां
समन्दहसितेक्षणां सशरचापपाशाङ्कुशाम् ।
अशेषजनमोहिनीमरुणमाल्यभूषाम्बरां
जपाकुसुमभासुरां जपविधौ स्मरेदम्बिकाम् ।।

sakuṅkuma vilepanāmalikacumbi
kastūrikāṁ samanda hasitekṣaṇāṁ
saśara cāpa pāśāṅkuśām
aśeṣajana mohinīṁ aruṇa mālya
bhūṣāmbarāṁ japākusuma bhāsurāṁ
japavidhau smaredambikām

I meditate on the Mother, whose eyes are smiling, who holds the arrow, bow, noose and the goad in Her hand. She is glittering with red garlands and ornaments. She is painted with kumkuma on her forehead and is red and tender like the japa flower.

Stotram 1000 Names

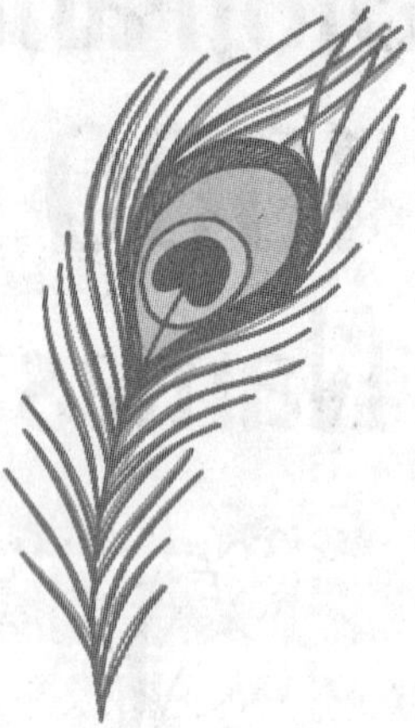

।। अथ श्रीललितासहस्रनामस्तोत्रम् ।।

श्रीमाता श्रीमहाराज्ञी
श्रीमत्-सिंहासनेश्वरी ।
चिदग्नि-कुण्ड-सम्भूता
देवकार्य-समुद्यता ।।१।।

atha śrīlalitāsahasranāmastotram

śrīmātā śrīmahārājñī
śrīmat-siṁhāsanēśvarī
cidagni-kunda-saṁbhūtā
dēvakārya-samudyatā (1)

1 **Srimatha**—Mother who gives immeasurable wealth who removes all sorrows and gives only happiness-indicates also her role of creation.

2 **Sri maharajni**—She who is the empress who takes care of the universe-indicates her role of protection.

3 **Sri math simasaneshwari**—She who sits on the throne of lions-indicates her role of destruction.

4 **Chidagni Kunda Sambootha**—She who rose from the fire of knowledge and is the ultimate truth.

5 **Deva karya samudhyatha**—She who is interested in helping devas.

उद्यद्भानु-सहस्राभा चतुर्बाहु-समन्विता ।
रागस्वरूप-पाशाढ्या क्रोधाकाराङ्कुशोज्ज्वला ।।२।।

udyadbhānu sahasrābhā
caturbāhusamanvitā
rāgasvarūpa pāśādhyā
krōdhākārāṅkuśōjjvalā (2)

6 **Udyath bhanu sahasrabha**—She who glitters like thousand rising suns.

7 **Chadur bahu samanvidha**—She who has four arms.

8 **Ragha Swaroopa pasadya**—She who has love for all in the form of rope (pasa)-She has this in one of her left hands.

9 **Krodhakarankusojwala**—She who glitters and has anger in the form of Anghusa–in one of her right hands.

मनोरूपेक्षु-कोदण्डा पञ्चतन्मात्र-सायका ।
निजारुण-प्रभापूर-मज्जद्ब्रह्माण्ड-मण्डला ।।३।।

manōrūpēkṣu kōdandā
pañcatanmātrasāyakā
nijārunaprabhāpūra majjad
brahmāndamandalā (3)

10 **Mano Rupeshu Kodanda**—She who has the bow of sweet cane which is her mind-in one of her left hands.

11 **Pancha than mathra sayaka**—"She who has five bows of touch, smell, hearing, taste and sight".

12 **Nijaruna prabha poora majjath brahmanda mandala**—She who makes all the universe immerse in her red colour which is like the sun in the dawn.

चम्पकाशोक-पुन्नाग-सौगन्धिक-लसत्कचा ।
कुरुविन्दमणि-श्रेणी-कनत्कोटीर-मण्डिता ।।४।।

campakāśōka
punnāgasaugandhikalasatkacā
kuruvindamaniśrēnī
kanat-kōtīramanditā (4)

13 **Champakasoka—punnaga-sowgandhika—lasath kacha**—"She who wears in her hair flowers like Champaka, Punnaga, and Sowgandhika".

14 **Kuru vinda mani—sreni-kanath kotira manditha**—She whose crown glitters with rows of inlaid precious stones (Padmaraga stones).

अष्टमीचन्द्र-विभ्राज-दलिकस्थल-शोभिता ।
मुखचन्द्र-कलङ्काभ-मृगनाभि-विशेषका ।।५।।

aṣtamīcandrabibhrāja
dalikasthalaśōbhitā
mukhacandrakalaṅkābha
mr̥ganābhiviśēṣakā (5)

15 **Ashtami chandra vibhraja—dhalika sthala shobhitha**—She who has a beautiful forehead like the half moon (visible on eighth day from new moon).

16 **Muka chandra kalankabha mriganabhi viseshaka**—She who has the tilaka (dot) of Musk in her forehead which is like the black shadow in the moon.

वदनस्मर-माङ्गल्य-गृहतोरण-चिल्लिका ।
वक्त्रलक्ष्मी-परीवाह-चलन्मीनाभ-लोचना ।।६।।

vadanasmaramāṁgalya
gr̥ hatōranacillikā
vaktralakṣmī
parīvāhacalanmīnābhalōcanā (6)

17 **Vadana smara mangalya griha thorana chillaka**—She who has beautiful eyelids which look like the ornaments to her face which is like cupids home.

18 **Vakthra lakshmi -parivaha-chalan meenabha lochana**—She who has beautiful eyes which look like fish in the pond of her face.

नवचम्पक-पुष्पाभ-नासादण्ड-विराजिता ।
ताराकान्ति-तिरस्कारि-नासाभरण-भासुरा ।।७।।

navacampakapuṣpābha
nāsādandavirājitā
tārākāntitiraskāri
nāsābharanabhāsurā (7)

19 **Nava champaka-pushpabha-nasa dhanda virajitha**—She who has nose like freshly opened flowers of Champaka.

20 **Thara kanthi thiraskari nasabharana bhasura**—She who has a nose ring which shines more than the star.

श्री

कदम्बमञ्जरी-कॢप्त-कर्णपूर-मनोहरा ।
ताटङ्क-युगली-भूत-तपनोडुप-मण्डला ॥८॥

kadaṁbamañjarīklipta
karnapūramanōharā
tātaṅkayugalībhūta
tapanōdupamandalā (8)

21 **Kadambha manjari kluptha karna poora manohara**—She who has beautiful ears like the kadamba flowers.

22 **Thadanga yugali bhootha thapanodupa mandala**—She who wears the sun and the moon as her ear studs.

पद्मराग-शिलादश-परिभावि-कपोलभूः ।
नवविद्रुम-बिम्बश्री-न्यक्कारि-रदनच्छदा ।।९।।

patmarāgaśilādarśa
paribhāvikapōlabhuh
navavidrumabiṁbaśrī
nyakkāriradanacchadā (9)

23 **Padma raga sila darsha paribhavika polabhu**—She who has cheeks which shine more than the mirror made of Padmaraga.

24 **Nava vidhruma bimbha sri nyakkari rathna chhadha**—She whose lips are like beautiful new corals.

शुद्ध-विद्याङ्कुराकार-द्विजपङ्क्ति-द्वयोज्ज्वला ।
कर्पूर-वीटिकामोद-समाकर्षि-दिगन्तरा ।।१०।।

śuddhavidyāṅkurākāra
dvijapaṅktidvayōjjvalā
karpūravītikāmōda
samākarṣaddigantarā (10)

25 **Shuddha vidyangurakara dwija pangthi dwayojjala**—She who has teeth which look like germinated true knowledge (Shodasakshari vidya).

26 **Karpoora Veedi Kamodha Samakarsha digandara**—She who chews betel leaf with the spices which give perfume in all directions.

निज-सल्लाप-माधुर्य-विनिर्भर्त्सित-कच्छपी ।
मन्दस्मित-प्रभापूर-मज्जत्कामेश-मानसा ॥११॥

nijasallāpamādhurya
vinirbhartsita kacchapī
mandasmitaprabhāpūra
majjatkāmēśamānasā (11)

27 **Nija Sallabha Madhurya Vinirbhardista Kacchabhi**—She who has voice sweeter than the notes produced by Sarawathi Devis Veena(This is called Kachabhi).

28 **Mandasmitha prabha poora majjat Kamesha manasa**—She who has lovely smile which is like the river in which the mind of cupid plays.

अनाकलित-सादृश्य-चुबुकश्री-विराजिता ।
कामेश-बद्ध-माङ्गल्य-सूत्र-शोभित-कन्धरा ।।१२।।

anākalitasādr̥ śya
cibukaśrīvirājitā
kāmēśabaddhamāṁgalya
sūtraśōbhitakandharā (12)

29 **Anakalidha Sadrushya Chibuka sri virajitha**—She who has a beautiful chin which has nothing else to compare.

30 **Kamesha baddha mangalya sutra shobitha kandhara**—She who shines with the sacred thread in her neck tied by Lord Kameshwara.

कनकाङ्गद-केयूर-कमनीय-भुजान्विता ।
रत्नग्रैवेय-चिन्ताक-लोल-मुक्ता-फलान्विता ॥१३॥

kanakāṁgadakēyūra
kamanīyabhujānvitā
ratnagraivēya
cintākalōlamuktāphalānvitā (13)

31 **Kankangadha Keyura Kamaniya Bujanvidha**—She who wears golden Armlets.

32 **Rathna graiveya chinthaka lola muktha phalanvitha**—She who wears necklace with moving pearls and dollar inlaid with gems.

कामेश्वर-प्रेमरत्न-मणि-प्रतिपण-स्तनी ।
नाभ्यालवाल-रोमालि-लता-फल-कुचद्वयी ।।१४।।

kāmēśvara
prēmaratnamanipratipanastanī
nābhyālavālarōmālī
latāphalakucadvayī (14)

33 **Kameswara prema rathna mani prathi pana sthani**—She who gave her breasts which are like the pot made of Rathna (precious stones) and has obtained the love of Kameshwara.

34 **Nabhyala vala Romali latha phala kucha dwayi**—She who has two breasts that are like fruits borne on the creeper of tiny hairs raising from her belly.

लक्ष्यरोम-लताधारता-समुन्नेय-मध्यमा ।
स्तनभार-दलन्मध्य-पट्टबन्ध-वलित्रया ॥१५॥

lakṣyarōmalatādhāratā
samunnēyamadhyamā
stanabhāradalanmadhya
pattabandhavalitrayā (15)

35 **Lakshya roma latha dharatha samunneya madhyama**—She who is suspected to have a waist because of the creeper like hairs raising from there.

36 **Sthana bhara dalan Madhya patta bhandha valithraya**—She who has three stripes in her belly which looks like having been created to protect her tiny waist from her heavy breasts.

अरुणारुण-कौसुम्भ-वस्त्र-भास्वत्-कटीतटी ।
रत्न-किङ्किणिका-रम्य-रशना-दाम-भूषिता ।।१६।।

arunārunakausuṁbha
vastrabhāsvatkatītati
ratnakiṅkinikāramya
raśanādāmabhūṣitā (16)

37 **Arunaruna kausumba vasthra bhaswat kati thati**—She who shines in her light reddish silk cloth worn over her tiny waist.

38 **Rathna kinkinika ramya rasana dhama bhooshitha**—She who wears a golden thread below her waist decorated with bells made of precious stones.

कामेश-ज्ञात-सौभाग्य-मार्दवोरु-द्वयान्विता ।
माणिक्य-मुकुटाकार-जानुद्वय-विराजिता ।।१७।।

kāmēśajñātasaubhāgya
mārdavōrudvayānvitā
mānikyamakutākāra
jānudvayavirājitā (17)

39 **Kamesha gnatha sowbhagya mardworu dwayanvitha**—She who has pretty and tender thighs known only to her consort, Kameshwara.

40 **Manikhya mukuta kara janu dwaya virajitha**—She who has knee joints like the crown made of manikya below her thighs.

इन्द्रगोप-परिक्षिप्त-स्मरतूणाभ-जङ्घिका ।
गूढगुल्फा कूर्मपृष्ठ-जयिष्णु-प्रपदान्विता ।।१८।।

indragōpaparikṣipta
smaratūnābhajaṅghikā
gūdhagūlphā kūrmapr̥ ṣtha
jayiṣnu prapadānvitā (18)

41 **Indra kopa parikshiptha smarathunabha jangika**—She who has forelegs like the cupids case of arrows followed by the bee called Indra kopa.

42 **Kooda Gulpha**—She who has round ankles.

43 **Koorma prashta jayishnu prapadanvidha**—She who has upper feet like the back of the tortoise.

नख-दीधिति-संछन्न-नमज्जन-तमोगुणा ।
पदद्वय-प्रभाजाल-पराकृत-सरोरुहा ।।१६।।

nakhadīdhitisaṁchanna
namajjanatamōgunā
padadvayaprabhājāla
parākr̥ tasarōruhā (19)

44 **Nakadhi dhithi samchanna namajjana thamoguna**—She who removes the darkness in the mind of her devotees by the sparkle of nails.

45 **Pada dwaya Prabha jala parakrutha saroruha**—She who has two feet which are much more beautiful than lotus flowers.

श्री

शिञ्जान-मणिमञ्जीर-मण्डित-श्री-पदाम्बुजा ।
मराली-मन्दगमना महालावण्य-शेवधिः ।।२०।।

śiñjānamanimañjīra
manditaśrīpadāṁbujā
marālīmandagamanā
mahālāvanyaśēvadhīh (20)

46 **Sinchana mani manjira manditha sri pamambuja**—She who has feet wearing musical anklets filled with gem stones.

47 **Marali Mandha Gamana**—She who has the slow gait like the swan.

48 **Maha Lavanya Sewadhi**—She who has the store house of supreme beauty.

सर्वारुणाऽनवद्याङ्गी सर्वाभरण-भूषिता ।
शिव-कामेश्वराङ्कस्था शिवा स्वाधीन-वल्लभा ।।२१।।

sarvārunānavadyāmgī
sarvābharanabhūṣitā
śivakāmēśvarāṅkasthā
śivā svādhīnavallabhā (21)

49 **Sarvaruna**—She who has light reddish colour of the dawn in all her aspects.

50 **Anavadhyangi**—She who has most beautiful limbs which do not lack any aspect of beauty.

51 **Srvabharana Bhooshita**—She who wears all the ornaments.

52 **Shivakameswarangastha**—She who sits on the lap of Kameshwara (Shiva).

53 **Shiva**—She who is the personification of Shiva.

54 **Swadheena Vallabha**—She who is the beloved of the Lord.

सुमेरु-मध्य-शृङ्गस्था श्रीमन्नगर-नायिका ।
चिन्तामणि-गृहान्तस्था पञ्च-ब्रह्मासन-स्थिता ।।२२।।

sumērumadhyaśṛ ṁgasthā
śrīmannagaranāyikā
cintāmanigṛ hāntasthā
pañcabrahmāsanasthitā (22)

55 **Summeru Madhya sringastha**—She who lives in the central peak of Mount Meru.

56 **Sriman nagara nayika**—She who is the chief of Srinagara (a town).

57 **Chinthamani grihanthastha**—She who lives in the all wish full filling house.

58 **Pancha brahmasana sthitha**—She who sits on the five brahmas viz., Brahma, Vishnu, Rudra, Esana, and Sadashiva.

महापद्‌माटवी-संस्था कदम्बवन-वासिनी ।
सुधासागर-मध्यस्था कामाक्षी कामदायिनी ।।२३।।

mahāpatmātavīsaṁsthā
kadaṁbavanavāsinī
sudhāsāgaramadhyasthā
kāmākṣīkāmadāyinī (23)

59 **Maha padma davi samstha**—She who lives in the forest of lotus flowers.

60 **Kadambha vana vasini**—She who lives in the forest of Kadmbha (Madurai city is also called Kadambha vana).

61 **Sudha sagara madhyastha**—She who lives in the middle of the sea of nectar.

62 **Kamakshi**—She who fulfills desires by her sight.

63 **Kamadhayini**—She who gives what is desired.

देवर्षि-गण-संघात-स्तूयमानात्म-वैभवा ।
भण्डासुर-वधोद्युक्त-शक्तिसेना-समन्विता ।।२४।।

dēvarṣiganasaṁghāta
stūyamānātmavaibhavā
bhandāsuravadhōdyukta
śaktisēnā samanvitā (24)

64 **Devarshi Gana-sangatha-stuyamanathma-vaibhava**—She who has all the qualities fit to be worshipped by sages and devas.

65 **Bhandasura vadodyuktha shakthi sena samavitha**—She who is surrounded by army set ready to kill Bandasura.

सम्पत्करी-समारूढ-सिन्धुर-व्रज-सेविता ।
अश्वारूढाधिष्ठिताश्व-कोटि-कोटिभिरावृता ।।२५।।

sampatkarīsamārūdha
sindhuravrajasēvitā
aśvārūdhādhiṣthitāśva
kōtikōtibhirāvṛtā (25)

66 **Sampathkari samarooda sindhoora vrija sevitha**—She who is surrounded by Sampathkari (that which gives wealth) elephant brigade.

67 **Aswaroodadishidaswa kodi kodi biravrutha**—She who is surrounded by crores of cavalry of horses.

चक्रराज-रथारूढ-सर्वायुध-परिष्कृता ।
गेयचक्र-रथारूढ-मन्त्रिणी-परिसेविता ।।२६।।

cakrarājarathārūdha
sarvāyudhapariṣkr̥ tā
gēyacakrarathārūdha
mantrinīparisēvitā (26)

68 **Chakra raja ratha rooda sarvayudha parishkridha**—She who is fully armed and rides in the Srichakra chariot with nine stories.

69 **Geya chakra ratha rooda manthrini pari sevitha**—She who rides in the chariot with seven stories and is served by manthrini who is the goddess of music.

किरिचक्र-रथारूढ-दण्डनाथा-पुरस्कृता ।
ज्वाला-मालिनिकाक्षिप्त-वह्निप्राकार-मध्यगा ॥२७॥

kiricakrarathārūdha
dandanāthāpuraskṛ tā
jvālāmālinikākṣipta
vahniprākāramadhyagā (27)

70 **Giri chakra ratharooda dhanda natha puraskrutha**—She who rides in the chariot with five stories and is served by goddess Varahi otherwise called Dhanda natha.

71 **Jwalimalika ksiptha vanhi prakara madhyaka**—She who is in the middle of the fort of fire built by the Goddess Jwalamalini.

भण्डसैन्य-वधोद्युक्त-शक्ति-विक्रम-हर्षिता ।
नित्या-पराक्रमाटोप-निरीक्षण-समुत्सुका ।।२८।।

bhandasainyavadhōdyukta
śaktivikramaharṣitā
nityāparākramātōpa
nirīkṣanasamutsukā (28)

72 **Bhanda sainya vadodyuktha shakthi vikrama harshitha**—She who was pleased by the various Shakthis (literally strength but a goddess) who helped in killing the army of Bhandasura.

73 **Nithya parakamatopa nireekshana samutsuka**—She who is interested and happy in observing the valour of Nithya devathas (literally goddess of every day).

भण्डपुत्र-वधोद्युक्त-बाला-विक्रम-नन्दिता ।
मन्त्रिण्यम्बा-विरचित-विषङ्ग-वध-तोषिता ।।२९।।

bhandaputravadhōdyukta
bālāvikramananditā
mantrinyaṁbāviracita
viṣaṁgavadhatōṣitā (29)

74 **Banda puthra vadodyuktha bala vikrama nandhita**—She who was pleased by the valour of Bala devi (her daughter) in destroying the sons of Banda.

75 **Manthrinyamba virachitha vishangavatha Doshitha**—She who became happy at seeing Goddess Manthrini kill Vishanga (this ogre brother of Banda) represents our desires for physical things).

विशुक्र-प्राणहरण-वाराही-वीर्य-नन्दिता ।
कामेश्वर-मुखालोक-कल्पित-श्रीगणेश्वरा ।।३०।।

viśukraprānaharana
vārāhīvīryananditā
kāmēśvaramukhālōka
kalpitaśrīganēśvarā (30)

76 **Vishuka prana harana varahi veeerya nandhitha**—She who appreciates the valour of Varahi in killing Vishuka (another brother of Banda who is a personification of ignorance).

77 **Kameshwara mukaloka kalpitha sri Ganeshwara**—"She who created God Ganesh by the mere look of the face of her Lord, Kameshwara".

महागणेश-निर्भिन्न-विघ्नयन्त्र-प्रहर्षिता ।
भण्डासुरेन्द्र-निर्मुक्त-शस्त्र-प्रत्यस्त्र-वर्षिणी ॥३१॥

mahāganēśanirbhinna
vighnayantrapraharṣitā
bhandāsurēndranir-mmukta
śastrapratyastravarṣinih (31)

78 **Mahaganesha nirbhinna vignayanthra praharshitha**—She who became pleased upon seeing Lord Ganesha destroy the Vigna Yantra (a contraption meant to cause delays).

79 **Banda surendra nirmuktha sashtra prathyasthra varshani**—She who rained arrows and replied with arrows against Bandasura.

करा‌ङ्गुलि-नखोत्पन्न-नारायण-दशाकृतिः ।
महा-पाशुपतास्त्राग्नि-निर्दग्धासुर-सैनिका ।।३२।।

karāṁgulinakhōtpanna
nārāyanadaśākṛ tih
mahāpāśupatāstrāgni
nirdagdhāsurasainikā (32)

80 **Karanguli nakhothpanna narayana dasakrithi**—She who created the ten avatharas of Narayana from the tip of her nails (when Bandasura send the Sarvasura asthra [arrow], she destroyed it by creating the ten avatharas of Vishnu).

81 **Mahapasupathasthragninirdagdhasura sainika**—She who destroyed the army of asuras by the Maha pasupatha arrow.

कामेश्वरास्त्र-निर्दग्ध-सभण्डासुर-शून्यका ।
ब्रह्मोपेन्द्र-महेन्द्रादि-देव-संस्तुत-वैभवा ।।३३।।

kāmēśvarāstranirdagddha
sabhandāsuraśūnyakā
brahmōpēndramahēndrādi
dēvasaṁstutavaibhavā (33)

82 **Kameshwarasthra nirdhagdha sabandasura sunyaka**—She who destroyed Bandasura and his city called Sunyaka by the Kameshwara arrow.

83 **Brhmopendra mahendradhi deva samsthutha vaibhava**—"She who is prayed by Lord Brahma, Vishnu, indra and other devas".

हर-नेत्राग्नि-संदग्ध-काम-संजीवनौषधिः ।
श्रीमद्वाग्भव-कूटैक-स्वरूप-मुख-पङ्कजा ।।३४।।

haranētrāgni- saṁdagdha
kāmasañjīvanauṣadhih
śrīmadvāgbhavakūtaika
svarūpamukhapaṅkajā (34)

84 **Hara nethragni sandhagdha kama sanjeevanoushadhi**—She who brought back to life the God of love Manmatha who was burnt to ashes by the fire from the eyes of Shiva.

85 **Sri vagbhave koodaiga swaroopa mukha pankaja**—She whose lotus face is Vagnhava Koota.

कण्ठाधः-कटि-पर्यन्त-मध्यकूट-स्वरूपिणी ।
शक्ति-कूटैकतापन्न-कट्यधोभाग-धारिणी ।।३५।।

kanthādhahkatiparyanta
madhyakūtasvarūpini
śaktikūtaikatāpanna
katyadhōbhāgadhārinī (35)

86 **Kantatha kadi paryantha Madhya koodaiga swaroopini**—She whose portion from neck to hips is Madya koota.

87 **Sakthi koodaiga thapanna Kadyatho bhaga dharini**—She whose portion below hips is the Shakthi koota.

मूल-मन्त्रात्मिका मूलकूटत्रय-कलेबरा ।
कुलामृतैक-रसिका कुलसंकेत-पालिनी ।।३६।।

mūlamantrātmikā
mūlakūtaṭrayakalēbarā
kulāmr̥ taikarasikā
kulasaṅkētapālinī (36)

88 **Moola manthrathmikha**—She who is the meaning of Moola manthra (root manthra) or She who is the cause.

89 **Moola kooda thraya kalebhara**—She whose body is the three parts of the basic manthra i.e. pancha dasakshari manthra.

90 **Kulamruthaika rasika**—She who enjoys the ecstatic state of oneness of one who sees, sight and what is seen or She who gets pleasure in drinking the nectar flowing from the thousand petalled lotus below the brain.

91 **Kula sanketha palini**—She who protects the sacred truths or symbols of the lineage.

कुलाङ्गना कुलान्तस्था कौलिनी कुलयोगिनी ।
अकुला समयान्तस्था समयाचार-तत्परा ।।३७।।

kulāṁganā kulāntasthā
kaulinīkulayōginī
akulā samayāntasthā
samayācāratatparā (37)

92 **Kulangana**—She who is a lady belonging to cultured family or She who is like Srividya known only to one whom it belongs.

93 **Kulanthastha**—She who is fit to be worshipped any where.

94 **Kaulini**—She who is the unification of the principles of Shiva and Shakthi.

95 **Kula yogini**—She who is related to the family or She who is related to the ultimate knowledge.

96 **Akula**—She who is beyond kula or She who is beyond any knowledge.

97 **Samayanthastha**—She who is within the mental worship of Shiva and Shakthi.

98 **Samayachara that para**—She who likes Samayachara i.e. worship stepwise from mooladhara Chakra.

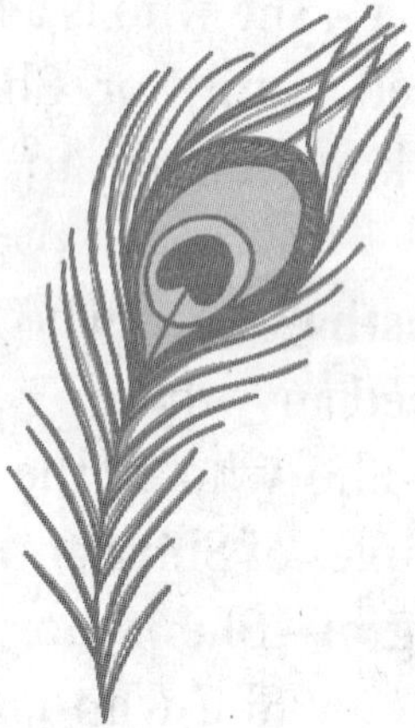

मूलाधारैक-निलया ब्रह्मग्रन्थि-विभेदिनी ।
मणि-पूरान्तरुदिता विष्णुग्रन्थि-विभेदिनी ।।३८।।

mūlādhāraikanilayā
brahmagranthivibhēdinī
manipūrāntaruditā
viṣnugranthivibhēdinī (38)

99 **Moladharaika nilaya**—She who exists in Mooladhara In Mooladhara which is in the form of four petalled lotus the kundalini sleeps.

100 **Brhama Grandhi Vibhedini**—She who breaks the tie in Brahma grandhi i.e she who helps us to cross the ties due to our birth.

101 **Mani poorantharudhitha**—She who exists in Mani pooraka chakra full dressed in her fineries.

102 **Vishnu grandhi vibedhini**—She who breaks the ties of Vishnu grandhi i.e., she who helps us cross the ties due to our position.

आज्ञा-चक्रान्तरालस्था रुद्रग्रन्थि-विभेदिनी ।
सहस्राराम्बुजारूढा सुधा-साराभिवर्षिणी ।।३६।।

ājñācakrāntarālasthā
rudragranthivibhēdinī
sahasrārāṁbujārūdhā
sudhāsārābhivarṣinī (39)

103 **Agna chakarantharalastha**—She who lives in between two eye lids in the form of she who orders.

104 **Rudra grandhi vibhedini**—She who breaks the ties of Rudra grandhi i.e she who helps us cross the ties due to our violent thoughts and nature.

105 **Saharারambhujarooda**—She who has climbed sahasrara the thousand petalled lotus which is the point of ultimate awakening.

106 Sudha sarabhi varshini—She who makes nectar flow in all our nerves from sahasrara i.e., she who gives the very pleasant experience of the ultimate.

तडिल्लता-समरुचिः षट्चक्रोपरि-संस्थिता ।
महासक्तिः कुण्डलिनी बिसतन्तु-तनीयसी ।।४०।।

tatillatāsamaruci
ṣatcakrōparisaṁsthitā
mahāsaktih kundalinī
bisatantutanīyasī (40)

107 **Thadillatha samaruchya**—She who shines like the streak of lightning.

108 **Shad chakropari samshitha**—She who is on the top of six wheels starting from mooladhara.

109 **Maha ssakthya**—She who likes worship by her devotees.

110 **Kundalini**—She who is in the form of Kundalini (a form which is a snake hissing and exists in mooladhara).

111 **Bisa thanthu thaniyasi**—She who is as thin as the thread from lotus.

भवानी भावनागम्या भवारण्य-कुठारिका ।
भद्रप्रिया भद्रमूर्ति भक्त-सौभाग्यदायिनी ।।४१।।

bhavānī bhāvanāgamyā
bhavāranyakuthārikā
bhadrapriyā bhadramūrti
bhaktasaubhāgyadāyinī (41)

112 **Bhavani**—She who gives life to the routine life of human beings or She who is the consort of Lord Shiva.

113 **Bhavana gamya**—She who can be attained by thinking.

114 **Bhavarany kudariga**—She who is like the axe used to cut the miserable life of the world.

115 **Bhadra priya**—She who is interested in doing good to her devotees.

116 **Bhadra moorthy**—She who is personification of all that is good.

117 **Bhaktha sowbhagya dhayini**—She who gives all good and luck to her devotees.

भक्तिप्रिया भक्तिगम्या भक्तिवश्या भयापहा ।
शाम्भवी शारदाराध्या शर्वाणी शर्मदायिनी ।।४२।

bhaktipriyā bhaktigamyā
bhaktivaśyā bhayāpahā
śāṁbhavī śāradārādhyā
śarvānī śarmadāyinī (42)

118 **Bhakthi priya**—She who likes devotion to her.

119 **Bhakthi gamya**—She who can be reached by devotion.

120 **Bhakthi vasya**—She who can be controlled by devotion.

121 **Bhayapaha**—She who removes fear.

122 **Sambhavya**—She who is married to Shambhu.

123 **Saradharadya**—She who is to be worshipped during Navarathri celebrated during autumn.

124 **Sarvani**—She who is the consort of Lord Shiva in the form of Sarvar.

125 **Sarmadhayini**—She who gives pleasures.

शाङ्करी श्रीकरी साध्वी शरच्चन्द्र-निभानना ।
शातोदरी शान्तिमती निराधारा निरञ्जना ।।४३।।

śāṅkarī śrīkarī sādhvī
śaraccandranibhānanā
śātōdarī śāntimatī
nirādhārā nirañjanā (43)

126 **Sankari**—She who is the consort of Sankara.

127 **Sreekari**—She who gives all forms of wealth and happiness.

128 **Sadhwi**—She who is eternally devoted to her husband.

129 **Sarat chandra nibhanana**—She who has the face like moon in the autumn.

130 **Satho dhari**—She who has a thin belly.

131 **Santhimathi**—She who is peace personified.

132 Niradhara—She who does not need any support to herself.

133 Niranjana—She who is devoid of any blemishes or scars.

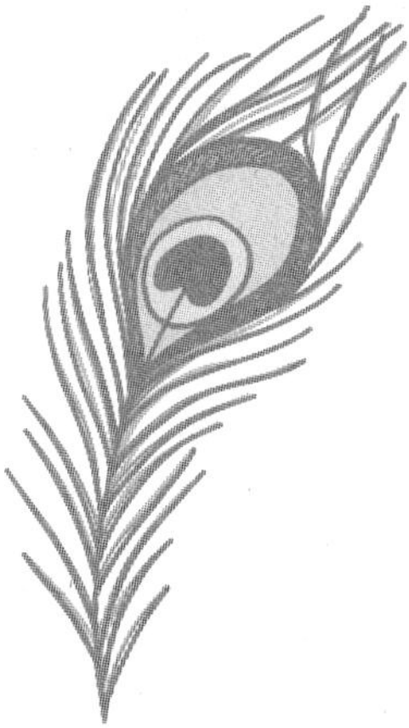

निर्लेपा निर्मला नित्या निराकारा निराकुला ।
निर्गुणा निष्कला शान्ता निष्कामा निरुपप्लवा ।।४४।।

nirlēpā nirmalā nityā
nirākārā nirākulā
nirgunā niṣkalā śāntā
niṣkāmā nirupaplavā (44)

134 **Nirlepa**—She who does not have any attachment.

135 **Nirmala**—She who is personification of clarity or She who is devoid of any dirt.

136 **Nithya**—She who is permanently stable.

137 **Nirakara**—She who does not have any shape.

138 **Nirakula**—She who cannot be attained by confused people.

139 **Nirguna**—She who is beyond any characteristics.

140 **Nishkala**—She who is not divided.

141 **Santha**—She who is peace.

142 **Nishkama**—She who does not have any desires.

143 **Niruppallava**—She who is never destroyed.

नित्यमुक्ता निर्विकारा निष्प्रपञ्चा निराश्रया ।
नित्यशुद्धा नित्यबुद्धा निरवद्या निरन्तरा ।।४५।।

nityamuktā nirvikārā
niṣprapañcā nirāśrayā
nityaśuddhā nityabuddhā
niravadyā nirantarā (45)

144 **Nithya muktha**—She who is forever free of the ties of the world.

145 **Nirvikara**—She never undergoes alteration.

146 **Nishprapancha**—She who is beyond this world.

147 **Nirasraya**—She who does not need support.

148 **Nithya shuddha**—She who is forever clean.

149 **Nithya bhuddha**—She who is for ever knowledge.

150 Niravadhya—She who can never be accused.

151 Niranthara—She who is forever continuous.

निष्कारणा निष्कलङ्का निरुपाधि निरीश्वरा ।
नीरागा रागमथनी निर्मदा मदनाशिनी ॥४६॥

niṣkāranā niṣkalaṅkā
nirupādhir- nirīśvarā
nīrāgā rāgamathanā
nirmadā madanāśinī (46)

152 **Nishkarana**—She who does not have cause.

153 **Nishkalanka**—She who does not have blemishes.

154 **Nirupadhi**—She who does not have basis.

155 **Nireeswara**—She who does not have any one controlling her.

156 **Neeraga**—She who does not have any desires.

157 **Ragha madhani**—She who removes desires from us.

158 **Nirmadha**—She who does not have any firm beliefs.

159 **Madhanasini**—She who destroys beliefs.

निश्चिन्ता निरहंकारा निर्मोहा मोहनाशिनी ।
निर्ममा ममताहन्त्री निष्पापा पापनाशिनी ।।४७।।

niścintā nirahaṅkārā
nirmōhā mōhanāśinī
nirmamā mamatāhantrī
niṣpāpā pāpanāśinī (47)

160 **Nischintha**—She who is not worried.

161 **Nirahankara**—She who does not have an ego.

162 **Nirmoha**—She who does not have any passion.

163 **Mohanasini**—She who destroys passion.

164 **Nirmama**—She who does not have selfish feelings.

165 **Mamatha hanthri**—She who destroys selfishness.

166 **Nishpapa**—She who does not have any sin.

167 **Papa nashini**—She who destroys sin.

निष्क्रोधा क्रोधशमनी निर्लोभा लोभनाशिनी ।
निःसंशया संशयघ्नी निर्भवा भवनाशिनी ॥४८॥

niṣkrōdhā krōdhaśamanī
nirlōbhā lōbhanāśinī
nissaṁśayā saṁśayaghnī
nirhavā bhavanāśinī (48)

168 **Nishkrodha**—She who is devoid of anger.

169 **Krodha—samani**—She who destroys anger.

170 **Nir Lobha**—She who is not miserly.

171 **Lobha nasini**—She who removes miserliness.

172 **Nissamsaya**—She who does not have any doubts.

173 **Samsayagni**—She who clears doubts.

174 **Nirbhava**—She who does not have another birth.

175 **Bhava nasini**—She who helps us not have another birth.

निर्विकल्पा निराबाधा निर्भेदा भेदनाशिनी ।
निर्नाशा मृत्युमथनी निष्क्रिया निष्परिग्रहा ।।४६।।

nirvikalpā nirābādhā
nirbhēdā bhēdanāśinī
nir-nnāśā mr̥ tyumathanī
niṣkriyā niṣparigrahā (49)

176 **Nirvikalpa**—She who does not do anything she does not desire.

177 **Nirabhadha**—She who is not affected by anything.

178 **Nirbhedha**—She who does not have any difference.

179 **Bhedha nasini**—She who promotes oneness.

180 **Nirnasa**—She who does not die.

181 **Mrityu madhani**—She who removes fear of death.

182 **Nishkriya**—She who does not have any work.

183 Nishparigraha—She who does not accept help from others.

निस्तुला नीलचिकुरा निरपाया निरत्यया ।
दुर्लभा दुर्गमा दुर्गा दुःखहन्त्री सुखप्रदा ।।५०।।

nistulā nīlacikurā
nirapāyā niratyayā
durlabhā durgamā durgā
duhkhahantrī sukhapradā (50)

184 **Nisthula**—She who does not have anything to be compared to.

185 **Neela chikura**—She who has dark black hair.

186 **Nirapaya**—She who is never destroyed.

187 **Nirathyaya**—She who does not cross limits of rules she herself created.

188 **Dhurlabha**—She who is difficult to obtain.

189 **Dhurgama**—She who can not be neared easily.

190 **Dhurga**—She who is Dhurga who is a nine year old girl.

191 **Dhuka hanthri**—She who removes sorrows.

192 **Sukha prada**—She who gives pleasures and happiness.

दुष्टदूरा दुराचार-शमनी दोषवर्जिता ।
सर्वज्ञा सान्द्रकरुणा समानाधिक-वर्जिता ।।५१।।

duṣtadūrā durācāraśamanī
dōṣavarjitā
sarvajñā sāndrakarunā
samānādhika varjitā (51)

193 **Dushta doora**—She who keeps far away from evil men.

194 **Durachara samani**—She who destroys evil practices.

195 **Dosha varjitha**—She who does not have anything bad.

196 **Sarvangna**—She who knows everything.

197 **Saandra karuna**—She who is full of mercy.

198 **Samanadhika varjitha**—She who is incomparable.

सर्वशक्तिमयी सर्व-मङ्गला सद्गतिप्रदा ।
सर्वेश्वरी सर्वमयी सर्वमन्त्र-स्वरूपिणी ॥५२॥

sarvaśaktimayī sarvamaṁgalā
sadgatipradā
sarvēśvarī sarvamayī
sarvamantra svarūpinī (52)

199 **Sarva shakthi mayi**—She who has personification of all strengths.

200 **Sarva mangala**—She who is personification of all that is good.

201 **Sad gathi prada**—She who gives us good path.

202 **Sarveshwari**—She who is goddess of all.

203 **Sarva mayi**—She who is everywhere.

204 **Sarva manthra swaroopini**—She who is personification of all manthras.

सर्व-यन्त्रात्मिका सर्व-तन्त्ररूपा मनोन्मनी ।
माहेश्वरी महादेवी महालक्ष्मीर्मृडप्रिया ।।५३।।

sarvayantrātmikā
sarvatantrarūpāmanōnmanī
māhēśvarī mahādēvī
mahālakṣmī mr̥ dapriyā (53)

205 **Sarva yanthrathmika**—She who is represented by all yantras (Talisman).

206 **Sarva thanthra roopa**—She who is also goddess of all Thanthras which is a method of worship.

207 **Manonmani**—She who is the result of mental thoughts of thoughts and actions.

208 **Maaheswari**—She who is the consort of Maheswara (Lord of everything).

209 **Mahaa devi**—She who is the consort of Mahe Deva (God of all gods).

210 Maha lakshmi—"She who takes the form of Mahalaksmi, the goddess of wealth".

211 Mrida priya—She who is dear to Mrida (a name of Lord Shiva).

महारूपा महापूज्या महापातक-नाशिनी ।
महामाया महासत्त्वा महाशक्तिर्महारतिः ॥५४॥

mahārūpā mahāpūjyā
mahāpātakanāśinī
mahāmāyā mahāsatvā
mahāśaktir- mahāratih (54)

212 **Maha roopa**—She who is very big.
213 **Maha poojya**—She who is fit to be worshipped by great people.
214 **Maha pathaka nasini**—She who destroys the major misdemeanors.
215 **Maha maya**—She who is the great illusion.
216 **Maha sathva**—She who is greatly knowledgeable.
217 **Maha sakthi**—She who is very strong.
218 **Maha rathi**—She who gives great happiness.

महाभोगा महैश्वर्या महावीर्या महाबला ।
महाबुद्धि महासिद्धि महायोगेश्वरेश्वरी ।।५५।।

mahābhōgā mahaiśvaryā
mahāvīryā mahābalā
mahābuddhir mahāsiddhir
mahāyōgīśvarēśvarī (55)

219 **Maha bhoga**—She who enjoys great pleasures.

220 **Mahaiswarya**—She who has great wealth.

221 **Maha veerya**—She who has great valour.

222 **Maha bala**—She who is very strong.

223 **Maha bhudhi**—She who is very intelligent.

224 **Maha sidhi**—She who has great super natural powers.

225 **Maha yogeswareswari**—She who is goddess of great yogis.

श्री

महातन्त्रा महामन्त्रा महायन्त्रा महासना ।
महायाग-क्रमाराध्या महाभैरव-पूजिता ॥५६॥

mahātantrā mahāmantrā
mahāyantrā mahāsanā
mahāyāgakramārādhyā
mahābhairavapūjitā (56)

226 **Mahathanthra**—She who has the greatest Thantra sasthras.

227 **Mahamanthra**—She who has the greatest manthras.

228 **Mahayanthra**—She who has the greatest yanthras.

229 **Mahasana**—She who has the greatest seat.

230 **Maha yaga kramaradhya**—She who should be worshipped by performing great sacrifices (Bhavana yaga and Chidagni Kunda yaga).

231 **Maha bhairava poojitha**—She who is being worshipped by the great Bhairava.

महेश्वर-महाकल्प-महाताण्डव-साक्षिणी ।
महाकामेश-महिषी महात्रिपुर-सुन्दरी ॥५७॥

mahēśvaramahākalpa
mahātāndavasākṣinī
mahākāmēśamahiṣī
mahātripurasundarī (57)

232 **Maheswara Mahakalpa Maha thandava sakshini**—She who will be the witness to the great dance to be performed by the great lord at the end of the worlds.

233 **Maha kamesha mahishi**—She who is the prime consort of the great Kameshwara.

234 **Maha tripura sundari**—She who is the beauty of the three great cities.

चतुःषष्ट्युपचाराढ्या चतुःषष्टिकलामयी ।
महाचतुः-षष्टिकोटि-योगिनी-गणसेविता ।।५८।।

catuhṣaṣtyupacārādhyā
catuhṣaṣtikalāmayī
mahācatuhṣaṣtikōti
yōginīganasēvitā (58)

235 **Chatustatyupacharadya**—She who should be worshipped with sixty four offerings.

236 **Chathu sashti kala mayi**—She who has sixty four sections.

237 **Maha Chathusashti kodi yogini gana sevitha**—She who is being worshipped by the sixty four crore yoginis in the nine different charkas.

मनुविद्या चन्द्रविद्या चन्द्रमण्डल-मध्यगा ।
चारुरूपा चारुहासा चारुचन्द्र-कलाधरा ॥५९॥

manuvidyā candravidyā
candramandalamadhyagā
cārurūpā cāruhāsā
cārucandrakalādharā (59)

238 **Manu Vidya**—She who is personification of Sri Vidya as expounded by Manu.

239 **Chandra Vidya**—She who is personification of Sri Vidya as expounded by Moon.

240 **Chandra mandala Madhyaga**—She who is in the center of the universe around the moon.

241 **Charu Roopa**—She who is very beautiful

242 **Charu Hasa**—She who has a beautiful smile.

243 **Charu Chandra Kaladhara**—She who wears the beautiful crescent.

श्री

चराचर-जगन्नाथा चक्रराज-निकेतना ।
पार्वती पद्मनयना पद्मराग-समप्रभा ।।६०।।

carācarajagannāthā
cakrarājanikētanā
pārvatī patmanayanā
patmarāgasamaprabhā (60)

244 **Charachara Jagannatha**—She who is the Lord of all moving and immobile things.

245 **Chakra Raja Nikethana**—She who lives in the middle of Sree Chakra.

246 **Parvathi**—She who is the daughter of the mountain.

247 **Padma nayana**—She who has eyes like the lotus.

248 **Padma raga samaprabha**—She who shines as much as the Padma Raga jewel.

पञ्च-प्रेतासनासीना पञ्चब्रह्म-स्वरूपिणी ।
चिन्मयी परमानन्दा विज्ञान-घनरूपिणी ॥६१॥

pañcaprētāsanāsīnā
pañcabrahmasvarūpinī
cinmayī paramānandā
vijñānaghanarūpinī (61)

249 **Pancha prethasana seena**—She who sits on the seat of five dead bodies (these are Brahma, Vishnu, Rudra, Eesa, and Sadasiva without their Shakthi [consort]).

250 **Pancha brahma swaroopini**—She who is personification of five brahmas (they are the gods mentioned in the last name with their Shakthi).

251 **Chinmayi**—She who is the personification action in every thing.

252 **Paramananda**—She who is supremely happy.

253 **Vignana Gana Roopini**—She who is the personification of knowledge based on science.

ध्यान-ध्यातृ-ध्येयरूपा धर्माधर्म-विवर्जिता ।
विश्वरूपा जागरिणी स्वपन्ती तैजसात्मिका ।।६२।।

dhyānadhyātṛ dhyēyarūpā
dharmādharmavivarjitā
viśvarūpā jāgarinī
svapantī taijasātmikā (62)

254 **Dhyana Dhyathru dhyeya roopa**—She who is personification of meditation, the being who meditates and what is being meditated upon.

255 **Dharmadhrama vivarjitha**—She who is beyond Dharma (justice) and Adharma (injustice).

256 **Viswa roopa**—She who has the form of the universe.

257 **Jagarini**—She who is always awake.

258 **Swapanthi**—She who is always in the state of dream.

259 **Thaijasathmika**—She who is the form of Thaijasa which is microbial concept.

सुप्ता प्राज्ञात्मिका तुर्या सर्वावस्था-विवर्जिता ।
सृष्टिकर्त्री ब्रह्मरूपा गोप्त्री गोविन्दरूपिणी ॥६३॥

suptā prājñātmikā turyā
sarvāvasthāvivarjitā
sr̥ ṣtikartrī brahmarūpā
gōptrī gōvindarūpinī (63)

260 **Suptha**—She who is in deep sleep.

261 **Prangnathmika**—She who is awake.

262 **Thurya**—She who is in trance.

263 **Sarvavastha vivarjitha**—She who is above all states.

264 **Srishti karthri**—She who creates.

265 **Brahma roopa**—She who is the personification of ultimate.

266 **Gopthri**—She who saves.

267 **Govinda roopini**—She who is of the form of Govinda.

संहारिणी रुद्ररूपा तिरोधान-करीश्वरी ।
सदाशिवाऽनुग्रहदा पञ्चकृत्य-परायणा ॥६४॥

samhārinī rudrarūpā
tirōdhānakarīśvarī
sadāśivānugrahadā
pañcakr̥ tyaparāyanā (64)

268 Samharini—She who destroys.

269 Rudhra roopa—She who is of the form of Rudhra.

270 Thirodhana kari—She who hides herself from us.

271 Eeswari—She who is of the form of easwara.

272 Sadashivaa—She who is of the form of Sadashiva.

273 Anugrahada—She who blesses.

274 Pancha krithya parayana—She who is engaged in the five duties of creation, existence, dissolving, disappearing, and blessing.

भानुमण्डल-मध्यस्था भैरवी भगमालिनी ।
पद्मासना भगवती पद्मनाभ-सहोदरी ।।६५।।

bhānumandalamadhyasthā
bhairavī bhagamālinī
patmāsanā bhagavatī
patmanābhasahōdarī (65)

275 **Bhanu mandala madhyastha**—She who is in the middle of the sun's universe.

276 **Bhairavi**—She who is the consort of Bhairava.

277 **Bhaga malini**—She who is the goddess bhaga malini.

278 **Padmasana**—She who sits on a lotus.

279 **Bhagavathi**—She who is with all wealth and knowledge.

280 **Padmanabha sahodari**—She who is the sister of Vishnu.

उन्मेष-निमिषोत्पन्न-विपन्न-भुवनावली ।
सहस्त्रशीर्षवदना सहस्राक्षी सहस्रपात् ।।६६।।

unmēṣanimiṣōtpanna
vipannabhuvanāvali
sahasraśīrṣavadanā
sahasrākṣī sahasrapāt (66)

281 **Unmesha nimishotpanna vipanna bhuvanavali**—She who creates and destroys the universe by opening and closing of her eye lids.

282 **Sahasra seersha vadana**—She who has thousands of faces and heads.

283 **Saharakshi**—She who has thousands of eyes.

284 **Sahasra path**—She who has thousands of feet.

आब्रह्म-कीट-जननी वर्णाश्रम-विधायिनी ।
निजाज्ञारूप-निगमा पुण्यापुण्य-फलप्रदा ।।६७।।

ābrahmakītajananī
varnāśramavidhāyinī
nijājñārūpanigamā
punyāpunyaphalapradā (67)

285 **Aabrahma keeda janani**—She has created all beings from worm to Lord Brahma.

286 **Varnashrama vidhayini**—She who created the four fold division of society.

287 **Nijangna roopa nigama**—She who gave orders which are based on Vedas.

288 **Punyapunya phala pradha**—She who gives compensation for sins and good deeds.

श्रुति-सीमन्त-सिन्दूरी-कृत-पादाब्ज-धूलिका ।
सकलागम-सन्दोह-शुक्ति-सम्पुट-मौक्तिका ।।६८।।

śrutisīmantasindūrīkr
tapādābjadhūlikā
sakalāgamasandōha
śuktisamputamauktikā (68)

289 **Sruthi seemantha kula sindhoori kritha padabjha dhooliga**—She whose dust from her lotus feet is the sindhoora fills up in the parting of the hair of the Vedic mother.

290 **Sakalagama sandoha shukthi samputa maukthika**—She who is like the pearl in the pearl holding shell of Vedas.

पुरुषार्थप्रदा पूर्णा भोगिनी भुवनेश्वरी ।
अम्बिकाऽनादि-निधना हरिब्रह्मेन्द्र-सेविता ।।६६।।

puruṣārthapradā pūrnā
bhōginī bhuvanēśvarī
aṁbikānādinidhanā
haribrahmēndrasēvitā (69)

291 **Purashartha pradha**—She who gives us the purusharthas of charity, assets, joy and moksha.

292 **Poorna**—She who is complete.

293 **Bhogini**—She who enjoys pleasures.

294 **Bhuvaneshwari**—She who is the Goddess presiding over the universe.

295 **Ambika**—She who is the mother of the world.

296 **Anadhi nidhana**—She who does not have either end or beginning.

297 **Hari brahmendra sevitha**—She who is served by Gods like Vishnu,Indra and Brahma.

नारायणी नादरूपा नामरूप-विवर्जिता ।
ह्रींकारी ह्रीमती हृद्या हेयोपादेय-वर्जिता ।।७०।।

nārāyanī nādarūpā
nāmarūpavivarjitā
hrīṅkārī hrīmatī hr̥ dyā
hēyōpādēya varjitā (70)

298 **Naarayani**—She who is like Narayana.

299 **Naada roopa**—She who is the shape of music (sound).

300 **Nama roopa vivarjitha**—She who does not have either name or shape.

301 **Hrim kari**—She who makes the holy sound Hrim.

302 **Harimathi**—She who is shy.

303 **Hrudya**—She who is in the heart (devotees).

304 **Heyopadeya varjitha**—She who does not have aspects which can be accepted or rejected.

राजराजार्चिता राज्ञी रम्या राजीवलोचना ।
रञ्जनी रमणी रस्या रणत्किङ्किणि-मेखला ।।७१।।

rājarājārcitā rājñī
ramyā rājīvalōcanā
rañjinī ramanī rasyā
ranatkiṅkinimēkhalā (71)

305 Raja rajarchitha—She who is being worshipped by king of kings.

306 Rakhini—She who is the queen of Kameshwara.

307 Ramya—She who makes others happy.

308 Rajeeva lochana—She who is lotus eyed.

309 Ranjani—She who by her red colour makes Shiva also red.

310 Ramani—She who plays with her devotees.

311 Rasya—She who feeds the juice of everything.

312 Ranath kinkini mekhala—She who wears the golden waist band with tinkling bells

रमा राकेन्दुवदना रतिरूपा रतिप्रिया ।
रक्षाकरी राक्षस घनी रामा रमणलम्पटा ।।७२।।

ramā rākēnduvadanā
ratirūpā ratipriyā
rakṣākarī rākṣasaghnī
rāmā ramanalampatā (72)

313 **Ramaa**—She who is like Lakshmi.

314 **Raakendu vadana**—She who has a face like the full moon.

315 **Rathi roopa**—She who attracts others with her features like Rathi (wife of God of love-Manmatha).

316 **Rathi priya**—She who likes Rathi.

317 **Rakshaa kari**—She who protects.

318 **Rakshasagni**—She who kills Rakshasas-ogres opposed to the heaven.

319 **Raamaa**—She who is feminine.

320 **Ramana lampata**—She who is interested in making love to her lord.

काम्या कामकलारूपा कदम्ब-कुसुम-प्रिया ।
कल्याणी जगतीकन्दा करुणा-रस-सागरा ।।७३।।

kāmyā kāmakalārūpā
kadaṁbakusumapriyā
kalyāṇī jagatīkandā
karuṇārasasāgarā (73)

321 **Kaamya**—She who is of the form of love.

322 **Kamakala roopa**—She who is the personification of the art of love.

323 **Kadambha kusuma priya**—She who likes the flowers of Kadamba.

324 **Kalyani**—She who does good.

325 **Jagathi kandha**—She who is like a root to the world.

326 **Karuna rasa sagara**—She who is the sea of the juice of mercy.

कलावती कलालापा कान्ता कादम्बरीप्रिया ।
वरदा वामनयना वारुणी-मद-विह्वला ।।७४।।

kalāvatī kalālāpā
kāntā kādaṁbarīpriyā
varadā vāmanayanā
vārunīmadavihvalā (74)

327 **Kalavathi**—She who is an artist or she who has crescents.

328 **Kalaalapa**—She whose talk is artful.

329 **Kaantha**—She who glitters.

330 **Kadambari priya**—She who likes the wine called Kadambari or She who likes long stories.

331 **Varadha**—She who gives boons.

332 **Vama nayana**—She who has beautiful eyes.

333 **Vaaruni madha vihwala**—She who gets drunk with the wine called varuni (The wine of happiness).

विश्वाधिका वेदवेद्या विन्ध्याचल-निवासिनी ।
विधात्री वेदजननी विष्णुमाया विलासिनी ।।७५।।

viśvādhikā vēdavēdyā
vindhyācalanivāsinī
vidhātrī vēdajananī
viṣnumāyā vilāsinī (75)

334 **Viswadhika**—She who is above all universe.

335 **Veda vedya**—She who can be understood by Vedas.

336 **Vindhyachala nivasini**—She who lives on Vindhya mountains.

337 **Vidhatri**—She who carries the world.

338 **Veda janani**—She who created the Vedas.

339 **Vishnu maya**—She who lives as the Vishnu maya.

340 **Vilasini**—She who enjoys love making.

क्षेत्रस्वरूपा क्षेत्रेशी क्षेत्र-क्षेत्रज्ञ-पालिनी ।
क्षयवृद्धि-विनिर्मुक्ता क्षेत्रपाल-समर्चिता ।।७६।।

kṣētrasvarūpā kṣētrēśī
kṣētrakṣētrajñapālinī
kṣayavr̥ ddhi vinirmuktā
kṣētrapālasamarcitā (76)

341 **Kshetra swaroopa**—She who is personification of the Kshetra or body.

342 **Kshetresi**—She who is goddess of bodies.

343 **Kshethra kshethragna palini**—She who looks after bodies and their lord.

344 **Kshaya vridhi nirmuktha**—She who neither decreases or increases.

345 **Kshetra pala samarchitha**—She who is worshipped by those who look after bodies.

विजया विमला वन्द्या वन्दारु-जन-वत्सला ।
वाग्वादिनी वामकेशी वह्निमण्डल-वासिनी ।।७७।।

vijayā vimalā vandyā
vandārujanavatsalā
vāgvādinī vāmakēśī
vahnimandalavāsinī (77)

346 **Vijaya**—She who is always victorious.

347 **Vimala**—She who is clean of ignorance and illusion.

348 **Vandhya**—She who is being worshipped by every body.

349 **Vandharu jana vatsala**—She who has affection towards all those who worship her.

350 **Vaag vadhini**—She who uses words with great effect in arguments.

351 **Vama kesi**—She who has beautiful hair.

352 **Vahni mandala vaasini**—She who lives in the universe of fire which is Mooladhara.

भक्तिमत्-कल्पलतिका पशुपाश-विमोचिनी ।
संहृताशेष-पाखण्डा सदाचार-प्रवर्तिका ।।७८।।

bhaktimatkalpalatikā
paśupāśavimōcinī
saṁhr̥ tāśēṣapāṣandā
sadācārapravartikā (78)

353 **Bhakthi mat kalpa lathika**—She who is the wish giving creeper Kalpaga.

354 **Pasu pasa vimochani**—She who removes shackles from the living.

355 **Samhrutha sesha pashanda**—She who destroys those people who have left their faith.

356 **Sadachara pravarthika**—She who makes things happen through good conduct.

तापत्रयाग्नि-सन्तप्त-समाह्लादन-चन्द्रिका ।
तरुणी तापसाराध्या तनुमध्या तमोऽपहा ।।७६।।

tāpatrayāgnisantapta
samāhlādanacandrikā
taruṇī tāpasārādhyā
tanumadhyā tamōpahā (79)

357 **Thapatryagni santhaptha samahladahna chandrika**—She who is like the pleasure giving moon to those who suffer from the three types of pain.

358 **Tharuni**—She who is ever young.

359 **Thapasa aradhya**—She who is being worshipped by sages.

360 **Thanu Madhya**—She who has a narrow middle (hip).

361 **Thamopaha**—She who destroys darkness.

चितिस्तत्पद-लक्ष्यार्था चिदेकरस-रूपिणी ।
स्वात्मानन्द-लवीभूत-ब्रह्माद्यानन्द-सन्ततिः ॥८०॥

citistatpadalakṣyārthā
cidēkarasarūpinī
svātmānandalavībhūta
brahmādyānandasantatīh (80)

362 **Chithi**—She who is personification of wisdom.

363 **Thatpada lakshyartha**—She who is the indicative meaning of the word 'thath' which is the first word of vedic saying 'that thou art'.

364 **Chidekara swaroopini**—She who is wisdom through out.

365 **Swathmananda lavi bhootha brahmadyanantha santhathi**—She who in her ocean of wisdom makes Wisdom about Brahmam look like a wave.

परा प्रत्यक्चितीरूपा पश्यन्ती परदेवता ।
मध्यमा वैखरीरूपा भक्त-मानस-हंसिका ।।८१।।

parā pratyakcitīrūpā
paśyantī paradēvatā
maddhyamā vaikharīrūpā
bhaktamānasahaṁsikā (81)

366 **Paraa**—She who is the outside meaning of every thing.

367 **Prathyak chidi roopa**—She who makes us look for wisdom inside.

368 **Pasyanthi**—She who sees everything within herself.

369 **Para devatha**—She who gives power to all gods.

370 **Madhyama**—She who is in the middle of everything.

371 **Vaikhari roopa**—She who is of the form with words.

372 **Bhaktha manasa hamsikha**—She who is like a swan in the lake called mind.

कामेश्वर-प्राणनाडी कृतज्ञा कामपूजिता ।
शृङ्गार-रस-सम्पूर्णा जया जालन्धर-स्थिता ।।८२।।

kāmēśvaraprānanādī
kr̥ tajñā kāmapūjitā
śr̥ ṁgārarasasampūrnā
jayā jālandharasthitā (82)

373 **Kameshwara prana nadi**—She who is the life source of Kameswara.

374 **Kruthagna**—She who watches all actions of every one or She who knows all.

375 **Kama poojitha**—She who is being worshipped by the god of love in the kama giri peeta of Mooladhara chakra-Kama.

376 **Srungara rasa sampoorna**—She who is lovely.

377 **Jayaa**—She who is personification of victory.

378 **Jalandhara sthitha**—She who is on Jalandhara peetha or She who is purest of the pure.

ओड्याणपीठ-निलया बिन्दु-मण्डलवासिनी ।
रहोयाग-क्रमाराध्या रहस्तर्पण-तर्पिता ।।८३।।

ōdhyānapīthanilayā
bindumandalavāsinī
rahōyāgakramārādhyā
rahastarpanatarpitā (83)

379 **Odyana peeda nilaya**—She who is on Odyana peetha or She who lives in orders

380 **Bindu mandala vaasini**—She who lives in the dot in the center of Srichakra.

381 **Raho yoga kramaradhya**—She who can be worshipped by secret sacrificial rites.

382 **Rahas tarpana tarpitha**—She who is pleased of chants knowing its meaning.

सद्यःप्रसादिनी विश्व-साक्षिणी साक्षिवर्जिता ।
षडङ्गदेवता-युक्ता षाड्गुण्य-परिपूरिता ।।८४।।

sadyahprasādinī
viśvasākṣinī sākṣivarjitā
ṣadaṁgadēvatāyuktā
ṣādgunyaparipūritā (84)

383 **Sadya prasadini**—She who is pleased immediately.

384 **Viswa sakshini**—She who is the witness for the universe.

385 **Sakshi varjitha**—She who does not have witness for herself.

386 **Shadanga devatha yuktha**—She who has her six parts as gods viz., heart, head, hair. Battle dress, eyes and arrows.

387 **Shadgunya paripooritha**—She who is full of six characteristics viz., wealth, duty, fame, knowledge, assets and renunciation.

नित्यक्लिन्ना निरुपमा निर्वाण-सुख-दायिनी ।
नित्या-षोडशिका-रूपा श्रीकण्ठार्ध-शरीरिणी ।।८५।।

nityaklinnā nirupamā
nirvānasukhadāyinī
nityāṣōdaśikārūpā
śrīkanthārdhaśarīrinī (85)

388 **Nithya klinna**—She in whose heart there is always mercy.

389 **Nirupama**—She who does not have anything to be compared to.

390 **Nirvanasukha dayini**—She who gives redemption.

391 **Nithya shodasika roopa**—She who is of the form sixteen goddesses.

392 **Sri kandartha sareerini**—She who occupies half the body of Lord Shiva.

प्रभावती प्रभारूपा प्रसिद्धा परमेश्वरी ।
मूलप्रकृर्ति अव्यक्ता व्यक्ताव्यक्त-स्वरूपिणी ।।८६।।

prabhāvatī prabhārūpā
prasiddhā paramēśvarī
mūlaprakṛ tiravyaktā
vyaktāvyaktasvarūpinī (86)

393 **Prabhavathi**—She who is lustrous of supernatural powers.

394 **Prabha roopa**—She who is personification of the light provided by super natural powers.

395 **Prasiddha**—She who is famous.

396 **Parameshwari**—She who is the ultimate goddess.

397 **Moola prakrithi**—She who is the root cause.

398 **Avyaktha**—She who is not clearly seen.

399 **Vyktha Avyaktha swaroopini**—She who is visible and not visible.

व्यापिनी विविधाकारा विद्याविद्या-स्वरूपिणी ।
महाकामेश-नयन-कुमुदाह्लाद-कौमुदी ॥८७॥

vyāpinī vividhākārā
vidyāvidyāsvarūpinī
mahākāmēśanayana
kumudāhlādakaumudi (87)

400 **Vyapini**—She who is spread everywhere.

401 **Vividhakara**—She who has several different forms.

402 **Vidhya avidhya swaroopini**—She who is the form of knowledge as well as ignorance.

403 **Maha kamesha nayana kumudahladha kaumudhi**—She who is like the full moon which opens the lotus like eyes of Lord Kameshwara.

भक्त-हार्द-तमोभेद-भानुमद्भानु-सन्ततिः ।
शिवदूती शिवाराध्या शिवमूर्तिः शिवङ्करी ।।८८।।

bhaktahārdatamōbhēda
bhānumadbhānusantatīh
śivadūtī śivārādhyā
śivamūrtīh śivaṅkarī (88)

404 **Bhaktha hardha thamo bedha bhanu mat bhanu santhathi**—She who is like the sun's rays which remove the darkness from the heart of devotees.

405 **Shivadhoothi**—She who sent Shiva as her representative.

406 **Shivaradhya**—She who is worshipped by Lord Shiva.

407 **Shiva moorthi**—She who is of the form of Lord Shiva.

408 **Shivangari**—She who makes good to happen.

शिवप्रिया शिवपरा शिष्टेष्टा शिष्टपूजिता ।
अप्रमेया स्वप्रकाशा मनोवाचामगोचरा ।।८९।।

śivapriyā śivaparā
śiṣṭēṣṭā śiṣṭapūjitā
aprамēyā svaprakāśā
manōvācāmagōcarā (89)

409 **Shiva priya**—She who is dear to Lord Shiva.

410 **Shivapara**—She who does not have any other interest except Lord Shiva.

411 **Shishteshta**—She who likes people with good habits.

412 **Shishta poojitha**—She who is being worshipped by good people.

413 **Aprameya**—She who cannot be measured.

414 **Swaprakasha**—She who has her own luster.

415 Mano vachama gochara—She who is beyond the mind and the word.

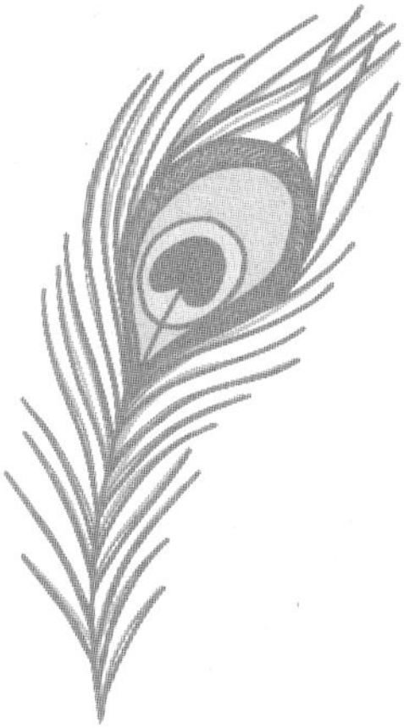

चिच्छक्तिश्चेतनारूपा जडशक्ति जडात्मिका ।
गायत्री व्याहृतिः सन्ध्या द्विजबृन्द-निषेविता ।।९०।।

cicchaktiścētanārūpā
jadaśaktir- jadātmikā
gāyatrī vyāhr̥ tih sandhyā
dvijavr̥ ndaniṣēvitā (90)

416 **Chitsakthi**—She who is the strength of holy knowledge.

417 **Chethana roopa**—She who is the personification of the power behind action.

418 **Jada shakthi**—She who is the strength of the immobile.

419 **Jadathmikha**—She who is the world of immobile.

420 **Gayathri**—She who is Gayathri.

421 **Vyahruthi**—She who is the grammar originating from letters.

422 **Sandhya**—She who is the union of souls and the God.

423 **Dwija brinda nishewitha**—She who is being worshipped by all beings.

तत्त्वासना तत्त्वमयी पञ्च-कोशान्तर-स्थिता ।
निस्सीम-महिमा नित्य-यौवना मदशालिनी ।।९१।।

tattvāsanā tattvamayī
pañcakōśāntarasthitā
nihsīmamahimā
nityayauvanā madaśālinī (91)

424 **Tatwasana**—She who sits on principles.
425 **Tat**—She who is that.
426 **Twam**—She who is you.
427 **Ayee**—She who is the mother.
428 **Pancha kosandara sthitha**—She who is in between the five holy parts.
429 **Nissema mahima**—She who has limitless fame.
430 **Nithya youawana**—She who is ever young.
431 **Madha shalini**—She who shines by her exuberance.

श्री

मदघूर्णित-रक्ताक्षी मदपाटल-गण्डभूः ।
चन्दन-द्रव-दिग्धाङ्गी चाम्पेय-कुसुम-प्रिया ।।९२।।

madaghūrnitaraktākṣī
madapātalagandabhūh
candanadravadigdhāṁgī
cāmpēya kusumapriyā (92)

432 **Madha goornitha rakthakshi**—She who has rotating red eyes due to her exuberance.

433 **Madha patala khandaboo**—She who has red cheeks due to excessive action.

434 **Chandana drava dhigdhangi**—She who applies sandal paste all over her body.

435 **Champeya kusuma priya**—She who likes the flowers of Champaka tree.

कुशला कोमलाकारा कुरुकुल्ला कुलेश्वरी ।
कुलकुण्डालया कौल-मार्ग-तत्पर-सेविता ।।९३।।

kuśalā kōmalākārā
kurukullā kulēśvarī
kulakundālayā
kaulamārgatatparasēvitā (93)

436 **Kusala**—She who is intelligent.

437 **Komalakara**—She who has soft beautiful form.

438 **Kuru kulla**—She who is of the form of Kuru kulla devi who lives in Vimarsa.

439 **Kuleshwari**—She who is the goddess for the clan.

440 **Kula kundalaya**—She who lives in kula kunda or She who is the power called Kundalani.

441 **Kaula marga that para sevitha**—She who is being worshipped by people who follow Kaula matha.

कुमार-गणनाथाम्बा
तुष्टिः पुर्ष्टि मर्ति धृतिः ।
शान्तिः स्वस्तिमती कार्न्ति
नन्दिनी विध्ननाशिनी ।।९४।।

kumāragananāthāṁbā
tuṣṭih puṣṭih matir-dhṛ tih
śāntih svastimatī kāntir
nandinī vighnanāśinī (94)

442 **Kumara gana nadambha**—She who is mother to Ganesha and Subrahmanya.

443 **Thushti**—She who is personification of happiness.

444 **Pushti**—She who is personification of health.

445 **Mathi**—She who is personification of wisdom.

446 **Dhrithi**—She who is personification of courage.

447 **Santhi**—She who is peaceful.

448 Swasthimathi—She who always keeps well.

449 Kanthi—She who is personification of light.

450 Nandhini—She who is personification of Nadhini daughter of Kama denu.

451 Vigna nasini—She who removes obstacles.

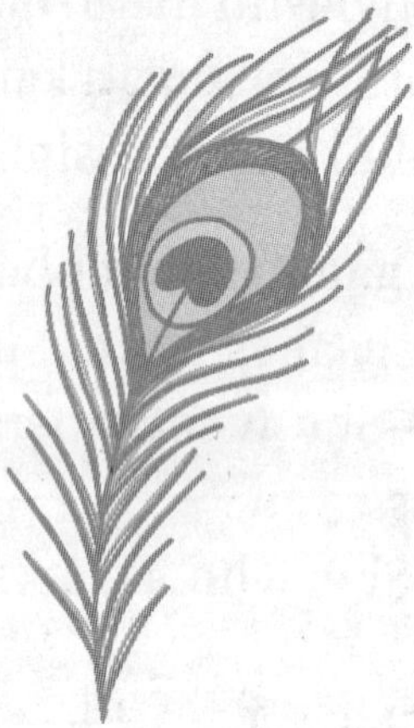

तेजोवती त्रिनयना लोलाक्षी-कामरूपिणी ।
मालिनी हंसिनी माता मलयाचल-वासिनी ।।९५।।

tējōvatī trinayanā
lōlākṣīkāmarūpinī
mālinī haṁsinī mātā
malayācalavāsinī (95)

452 **Tejowathi**—She who shines.

453 **Trinayana**—She who has three eyes.

454 **Lolakshi-Kamaroopini**—She who has wandering passionate eyes.

455 **Malini**—She who wears a garland.

456 **Hamsini**—She who is surrounded by swans.

457 **Matha**—She who is the mother.

458 **Malayachala vasini**—She who lives in the Malaya mountain.

सुमुखी नलिनी सुभ्रूः शोभना सुरनायिका ।
कालकण्ठी कान्तिमती क्षोभिणी सूक्ष्मरूपिणी ।।९६।।

sumukhī nalinī subhrūh
śōbhanā suranāyikā
kālakanthī kāntimatī
kṣōbhinī sūkṣmarūpinī (96)

459 **Sumukhi**—She who has a pleasing disposition.

460 **Nalini**—She who is tender.

461 **Subru**—She who has beautiful eyelids.

462 **Shobhana**—She who brings good things.

463 **Sura Nayika**—She who is the leader of devas.

464 **Kala kanti**—She who is the consort of he who killed the god of death.

465 **Kanthi mathi**—She who has ethereal luster.

466 **Kshobhini**—She who creates high emotions or She who gets agitated.

467 **Sukshma roopini**—She who has a micro stature.

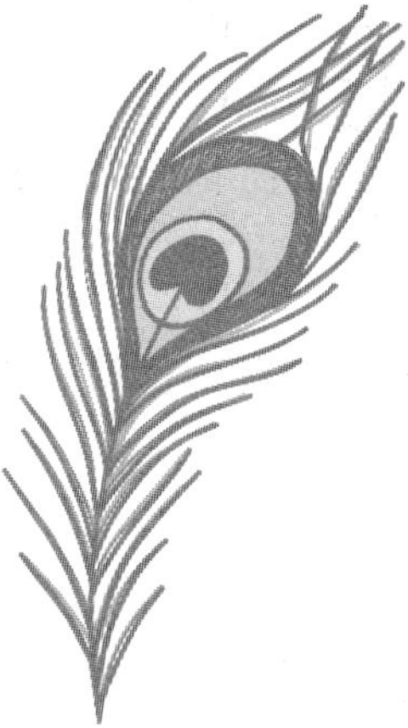

वज्रेश्वरी वामदेवी वयोऽवस्था-विवर्जिता ।
सिद्धेश्वरी सिद्धविद्या सिद्धमाता यशस्विनी ।।९७।।

vajrēśvarī vāmadēvī
vayōvasthā vivarjitā
siddhēśvarī siddhavidyā
siddhamātā yaśasvinī (97)

468 **Vajreshwari**—She who is Vajreswari (lord of diamonds) who occupies jalandhara peetha.

469 **Vamadevi**—She who is the consort of Vama deva.

470 **Vayovastha vivarjitha**—She who does not change with age.

471 **Sidheswari**—She who is the goddess of Siddhas (saints with super natural powers).

472 **Sidha vidya**—She who is personification of pancha dasa manthra which is called siddha vidya.

473 Sidha matha—She who is the mother of Siddhas.

474 Yasawini—She who is famous.

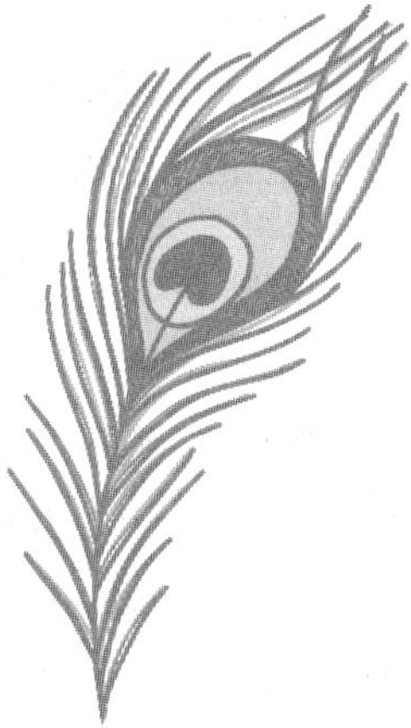

विशुद्धिचक्र-निलयाऽऽरक्तवर्णा त्रिलोचना ।
खट्वाङ्गादि-प्रहरणा वदनैक-समन्विता ।।९८।।

viśuddhicakranilayā
raktavarnā trilōcanā
khatvāṁgādipraharanā
vadanaikasamanvitā (98)

475 **Vishudhichakra Nilaya**—She who is in sixteen petalled lotus.

476 **Aarakthavarni**—She who is slightly red.

477 **Trilochana**—She who has three eyes.

478 **Khadwangadhi prakarana**—She who has arms like the sword.

479 **Vadanaika samavidha**—She who has one face.

पायसान्नप्रिया त्वक्स्था पशुलोक-भयङ्करी ।
अमृतादि-महाशक्ति-संवृता डाकिनीश्वरी ।।९९।।

pāyasānnapriyā tvaksthā
paśulōkabhayaṅkarī
amṛ tādimahāśaktisaṁvṛ tā
dākinīśvarī (99)

480 **Payasanna priya**—She who likes sweet rice (Payasam).

481 **Twakstha**—She who lives in the sensibility of the skin.

482 **Pasu loka Bhayamkari**—She who creates fear for animal like men.

483 **Amruthathi maha sakthi samvrutha**—She who is surrounded by Maha shakthis like Amrutha, Karshini, Indrani, Eesani, uma, Urdwa kesi.

484 **Dakineeswari**—She who is goddess of the south (denoting death).

अनाहताब्ज-निलया श्यामाभा वदनद्वया ।
दंष्ट्रोज्ज्वलाऽक्ष-मालादि-धरा रुधिरसंस्थिता ॥१००॥

anāhatābjanilayā
śyāmābhā vadanadvayā
daṁṣtrōjjvalākṣamālādidharā
rudhirasaṁsthitā (100)

485 **Anahathabja nilaya**—She who lives in the twelve petalled lotus.

486 **Syamabha**—She who is greenish black.

487 **Vadanadwaya**—She who has two faces.

488 **Dhamshtrojwala**—She who shines with long protruding teeth.

489 **Aksha maladhi dhara**—She who wears meditation chains.

490 **Rudhira samsthida**—She who is in blood.

कालरात्र्यादि-शक्त्यौघ-वृता स्निग्धौदनप्रिया ।
महावीरेन्द्र-वरदा राकिण्यम्बा-स्वरूपिणी ।।१०१।।

kālarātryādiśaktyaughavr̥ tā
snigdhaudanapriyā
mahāvīrēndravaradā
rākinyaṁbāsvarūpinī (101)

491 Kalarathryadhi Shakthi yougavrudha—She who is surrounded by Shakthis like Kalarathri. Kanditha, Gayathri, ...etc.

492 Sniggdowdhana priya—She who likes Ghee mixed rice.

493 Maha veerendra varadha—She who gives boons to great heroes or She who gives boons to great sages.

494 Rakinyambha swaroopini—She who has names like rakini.

मणिपूराब्ज-निलया वदनत्रय-संयुता ।
वज्रादिकायुधोपेता डामर्यादिभिरावृता ।।१०२।।

manipūrābjanilayā
vadanatrayasaṁyutā
vajrādikāyudhōpētā
dāmaryādibhirāvr̥ tā (102)

495 **Mani poorabja nilaya**—She who lives in ten petalled lotus.

496 **Vadana thraya samyudha**—She who has three faces.

497 **Vajradhikayudhopetha**—She who has weapons like Vajrayudha.

498 **Damaryadhibhi ravrutha**—She who is surrounded by Goddess like Damari.

रक्तवर्णा मांसनिष्ठा गुडान्न-प्रीत-मानसा ।
समस्तभक्त-सुखदा लाकिन्यम्बा-स्वरूपिणी ।।१०३।।

raktavarnā māṁsaniṣṭhā
gudānnaprītamānasā
samastabhaktasukhadā
lākinyaṁbāsvarūpinī (103)

499 **Raktha varna**—She who is of the colour of blood.

500 **Mamsa nishta**—She who is in flesh.

501 **Gudanna preetha manasa**—She who likes rice mixed with jaggery.

502 **Samastha bhaktha sukhadha**—She who gives pleasure to all her devotees.

503 **Lakinyambha swaroopini**—She who is famous in the name of 'Lakini'.

स्वाधिष्ठानाम्बुज-गता चतुर्वक्त्रमनोहरा ।
शूलाद्यायुध-सम्पन्ना पीतवर्णाऽतिगर्विता ।।१०४।।

svādhiṣṭhānāṁbujagatā
catur-vaktramanōharā
śūlādyāyudhasampannā
pītavarnātigarvitā (104)

504 **Swadhishtanambujagatha**—She who lives in the six petalled lotus.

505 **Chathur vakthra manohara**—She who has four beautiful faces.

506 **Sulayudha sampanna**—She who has weapons like Spear.

507 **Peetha varna**—She who is of golden colour.

508 **Adhi garvitha**—She who is very proud.

मेदोनिष्ठा मधुप्रीता बन्धिन्यादि-समन्विता ।
दध्यन्नासक्त-हृदया काकिनी-रूप-धारिणी ।।१०५।।

mēdōniṣṭhā madhuprītā
bandinyādisamanvitā
dadhyannāsaktahr̥ dayā
kākinīrūpadhārinī (105)

509 **Medho nishta**—She who is in the fatty layer.

510 **Madhu preetha**—She who likes honey.

511 **Bhandinyadhi samanvidha**—She who is surrounded by Shakthis called Bandhini.

512 **Dhadyanna saktha hridhaya**—She who likes curd rice.

513 **Kakini roopa dharini**—She who resembles 'Kakini'.

मूलाधाराम्बुजारूढा पञ्च-वक्त्राऽस्थि-संस्थिता ।
अङ्कुशादि-प्रहरणा वरदादि-निषेविता ।।१०६।।

mūlādhārāṁbujārūdhā
pañcavaktrāsthisaṁsthitā
aṅkuśādipraharanā
varadādiniṣēvitā (106)

514 **Mooladrambujarooda**—She who sits on the mooladhara kamala or the lotus which is the basic support.

515 **Pancha vakthra**—She who has five faces.

516 **Sthithi samsthitha**—She who is in the bones.

517 **Ankusathi praharana**—She who holds Ankusha and other weapons.

518 **Varadadhi nishevitha**—She who is surrounded by Vardha and other shakthis.

मुद्गौदनासक्त-चित्ता साकिन्यम्बा-स्वरूपिणी ।
आज्ञा-चक्राब्ज-निलया शुक्लवर्णा षडानना ।।१०७।।

mudgaudanāsaktacittā
sākinyaṁbāsvarūpinī
ājñācakrābjanilayā
śuklavarnā ṣadānanā (107)

519 **Mudgou danasaktha chittha**—She who likes rice mixed with green gram dhal.

520 **Sakinyambha swaroopini**—She who has the name 'Sakini'.

521 **Agna chakrabja nilaya**—She who sits on the lotus called Agna chakra or the wheel of order.

522 **Shukla varna**—She who is white coloured.

523 **Shadanana**—She who has six faces.

मज्जासंस्था हंसवती-मुख्य-शक्ति-समन्विता ।
हरिद्रान्नैक-रसिका हाकिनी-रूप-धारिणी ।।१०८।।

majjāsaṁsthā haṁsavatī
mukhyaśaktisamanvitā
haridrānnaikarasikā
hākinīrūpadhāriṇī (108)

524 **Majja samstha**—She who is in the fat surrounding the body.

525 **Hamsavathi mukhya shakthi samanvitha**—She who is surrounded by shakthis called Hamsavathi.

526 **Hardrannaika rasika**—She who likes rice mixed with turmeric powder.

527 **Hakini roopa dharini**—She who has the name 'Hakini'.

सहस्रदल-पद्मस्था सर्व-वर्णोप-शोभिता ।
सर्वायुधधरा शुक्ल-संस्थिता सर्वतोमुखी ।।१०६।।

sahasradalapatmasthā
sarvavarnōpaśōbhitā
sarvāyudhadharā
śuklasaṁsthitā sarvatōmukhī (109)

528 **Sahasra dhala padhmastha**—She who sits on thousand petalled lotus.

529 **Sarva varnopi shobitha**—She who shines in all colours.

530 **Sarvayudha dhara**—She who is armed with all weapons.

531 **Shukla samsthitha**—She who is in shukla or semen.

532 **Sarvathomukhi**—She who has faces everywhere.

सर्वौदन-प्रीतचित्ता याकिन्यम्बा-स्वरूपिणी ।
स्वाहा स्वधाऽमर्ति मेधा श्रुतिः स्मृर्ति अनुत्तमा ।।११०।।

sarvaudanaprītacittā
yākinyambāsvarūpinī
svāhāsvadhāmatir-mēdhā
śrutismṛ tiranuttamā (110)

533 **Sarvou dhana preetha chittha**—She who likes all types of rice.

534 **Yakinyambha swaroopini**—She who is named as 'yakini'.

535 **Swaha**—She who is personification of Swaha (the manthra chanted during fire sacrifice).

536 **Swadha**—She who is of the form of Swadha.

537 **Amathi**—She who is ignorance.

538 **Medha**—She who is knowledge.

539 **Sruthi**—She who is Vedas.

540 **Smrithi**—She who is the guide to Vedas.

541 **Anuthama**—She who is above all.

पुण्यकीर्तिः पुण्यलभ्या पुण्यश्रवण-कीर्तना ।
पुलोमजार्चिता बन्ध-मोचनी बन्धुरालका ।१११।।

punyakīrtih punyalabhyā
punyaśravanakīrtanā
pulōmajār-ccitā
bandhamōcinī barbbarālakā (111)

542 Punya keerthi—She who is famous for good deeds.

543 Punya labhya—She who can be attained by good deeds.

544 Punya sravana keerthana—She who gives good for those who listen and those who sing about her.

545 Pulomajarchidha—She who is worshipped by wife of Indra.

546 Bandha mochini—She who releases us from bondage.

547 Barbharalaka—She who has forelocks which resembles waves.

विमर्शरूपिणी विद्या वियदादि-जगत्प्रसूः ।
सर्वव्याधि-प्रशमनी सर्वमृत्यु-निवारिणी ।।११२।।

vimarśarūpinī
vidyāviyadādijagatprasū
sarvavyādhipraśamanī
sarvamr̥ tyunivārinī (112)

548 Vimarsa roopini—She who is hidden from view.

549 Vidhya—She who is 'learning'.

550 Viyadhadhi jagat prasu—She who created the earth and the sky.

551 Sarva vyadhi prasamani—She who cures all diseases.

552 Sarva mrutyu nivarini—She who avoids all types of death.

अग्रगण्याऽचिन्त्यरूपा कलिकल्मष-नाशिनी ।
कात्यायनी कालहन्त्री कमलाक्ष-निषेविता ।।११३।।

agraganyācintyarūpā
kalikanmaṣanāśinī
kātyāyanī kālahantrī
kamalākṣaniṣēvitā (113)

553 **Agra ganya**—She who is at the top.

554 **Achintya roopa**—She who is beyond thought.

555 **Kali kalmasha nasini**—She who removes the ills of the dark age.

556 **Kathyayini**—She who is Kathyayini in Odyana peetha or She who is the daughter of sage Kathyayana.

557 **Kala hanthri**—She who kills god of death.

558 **Kamalaksha nishevitha**—She who is being worshipped by the lotus eyed Vishnu.

ताम्बूल-पूरित-मुखी दाडिमी-कुसुम-प्रभा ।
मृगाक्षी मोहिनी मुख्या मृडानी मित्ररूपिणी ।।११४।।

tāṁbūlapūritamukhī
dādimīkusumaprabhā
mr̥ gākṣī mōhinīmukhyā
mr̥ dānī mitrarūpinī (114)

559 **Thamboola pooritha mukhi**—'She whose mouth is filled with betel leaves, betel nut and lime'.

560 **Dhadimi kusuma prabha**—She whose colour is like the pomegranate bud.

561 **Mrgakshi**—She who has eyes like deer.

562 **Mohini**—She who bewitches.

563 **Mukhya**—She who is the chief.

564 **Mridani**—She who gives pleasure.

565 **Mithra roopini**—She who is of the form of Sun.

नित्यतृप्ता भक्तनिधि नियन्त्री निखिलेश्वरी ।
मैत्र्यादि-वासनालभ्या महाप्रलय-साक्षिणी ।।११५।।

nityatr̥ ptā bhaktanidhir
niyantrī nikhilēśvarī
maitryādivāsanālabhyā
mahāpralayasākṣinī (115)

566 **Nithya Truptha**—She who is satisfied always.

567 **Bhaktha Nidhi**—She who is the treasure house of devotees.

568 **Niyanthri**—She who controls.

569 **Nikhileswari**—She who is goddess for every thing.

570 **Maitryadhi vasana Labhya**—She who can be attained by habits like Maithree (friendship).

571 **Maha pralaya sakshini**—She who is the witness to the great deluge.

परा शक्तिः परा निष्ठा प्रज्ञानघन-रूपिणी ।
माध्वीपानालसा मत्ता मातृका-वर्ण-रूपिणी ।।११६।।

parāśaktih parāniṣṭhā
prajñānaghanarūpinī
mādhvīpānālasā mattā
mātṛ kāvar-nnarūpinī (116)

572 **Para Shakthi**—She who is the end strength.

573 **Para Nishta**—She who is at the end of concentration.

574 **Prgnana Gana roopini**—She who is personification of all superior knowledge.

575 **Madhvi pana lasaa**—She who is not interested in anything else due to drinking of toddy.

576 **Matha**—She who appears to be fainted.

577 **Mathruka varna roopini**—She who is the model of colour and shape.

महाकैलास-निलया मृणाल-मृदु-दोर्लता ।
महनीया दयामूर्तिः महासाम्राज्य-शालिनी ।।११७।।

mahākailāsanilayā
mr̥ nālamr̥ dudōrlatā
mahanīyā dayāmūrtih
mahāsāmrājyaśālinī (117)

578 **Maha Kailasa nilaya**—She who sits on Maha Kailasa.

579 **Mrinala mrudhu dhorllatha**—She who has arms as tender as lotus stalk.

580 **Mahaneeya**—She who is fit to be venerated.

581 **Dhaya moorthi**—She who is personification of mercy.

582 **Maha samrajya shalini**—She who is the chef of all the worlds.

आत्मविद्या महाविद्या श्रीविद्या कामसेविता ।
श्री-षोडशाक्षरी-विद्या त्रिकूटा कामकोटिका ॥११८॥

ātmavidyā mahāvidyā
śrīvidyā kāmasēvitā
śrīṣōdaśākṣarīvidyā
trikūtā kāmakōtikā (118)

583 **Atma vidhya**—She who is the science of soul.

584 **Maha Vidhya**—She who is the great knowledge.

585 **Srividhya**—She who is the knowledge of Goddess.

586 **Kama sevitha**—She who is worshipped by Kama, the God of love.

587 **Sri Shodasakshari vidhya**—She who is the sixteen lettered knowledge.

588 **Trikoota**—She who is divided in to three parts.

589 **Kama Kotika**—She who sits on Kama Koti peetha.

कटाक्ष-किङ्करी-भूत-कमला-कोटि-सेविता ।
शिरःस्थिता चन्द्रनिभा भालस्थेन्द्र-धनुःप्रभा ।।११६।।

katākṣakiṅkarībhūta
kamalākōtisēvitā
śiraḥsthitā candranibhā
phālasēthandra dhanuprabhā (119)

590 **Kataksha kimkari bhootha kamala koti sevitha**—She who is attended by crores of Lakshmis who yearn for her simple glance.

591 **Shira sthitha**—She who is in the head.

592 **Chandra nibha**—She who is like the full moon.

593 **Bhalastha**—She who is in the forehead.

594 **Indra Dhanu Prabha**—She who is like the rain bow.

श्री

हृदयस्था रविप्रख्या त्रिकोणान्तर-दीपिका ।
दाक्षायणी दैत्यहन्त्री दक्षयज्ञ-विनाशिनी ॥१२०॥

hṛ dayasthā raviprakhyā
trikōnāntaradīpikā
dākṣāyanī daityahantrī
dakṣayajñavināśinī (120)

595 **Hridayastha**—She who is in the heart.

596 **Ravi pragya**—She who has luster like Sun God.

597 **Tri konanthara deepika**—She who is like a light in a triangle.

598 **Dakshayani**—She who is the daughter of Daksha.

599 **Dhithya hanthri**—She who kills asuras.

600 **Daksha yagna vinasini**—She who destroyed the sacrifice of Rudra.

दरान्दोलित-दीर्घाक्षी दर-हासोज्ज्वलन्-मुखी ।
गुरुमूर्तिर्गुणनिधिर्गोमाता गुहजन्मभूः ।।१२१।।

darāndōlitadīrghākṣī
darahāsōjjvalanmukhī
gurūmūrtir-gunanidhir
gōmātā guhajanmabhūh (121)

601 **Dharandholitha deergakshi**—She who has long eyes which have slight movement.

602 **Dharahasojwalanmukhi**—She who has face that glitters with her smile.

603 **Guru moorthi**—She who is the teacher.

604 **Guna nidhi**—She who is the treasure house of good qualities.

605 **Gomatha**—She who is the mother cow.

606 **Guhajanma bhoo**—She who is the birth place of Lord Subrahmanya.

देवेशी दण्डनीतिस्था दहराकाश-रूपिणी ।
प्रतिपन्मुख्य-राकान्त-तिथि-मण्डल-पूजिता ॥१२२॥

dēvēśī danītisthā
daharākāśarūpinī
pratipanmukhyarākānta
tithimandalapūjitā (122)

607 **Deveshi**—She who is the goddess of Gods.

608 **Dhanda neethistha**—She who judges and punishes.

609 **Dhaharakasa roopini**—She who is of the form of wide sky.

610 **Prathi panmukhya rakantha thidhi mandala poojitha**—She who is being worshipped on all the fifteen days from full moon to new moon.

कलात्मिका कलानाथा काव्यालाप-विनोदिनी ।
सचामर-रमा-वाणी-सव्य-दक्षिण-सेविता ।।१२३।।

kalātmikā kalānāthā
kāvyālāpavinōdinī
sacāmararamāvānī
savyadakṣinasēvitā (123)

611 **Kalathmika**—She who is the soul of arts.

612 **Kala nadha**—She who is the chief of arts.

613 **Kavya labha vimodhini**—She who enjoys being described in epics.

614 **Sachamara rama vani savya dhakshina sevitha**—She who is being fanned by Lakshmi the goddess of wealth and Saraswathi the goddess of knowledge.

आदिशक्तिरमेयात्मा परमा पावनाकृतिः ।
अनेककोटि-ब्रह्माण्ड-जननी दिव्यविग्रहा ।।१२४।।

ādiśaktiramēyātmā
paramāpāvanākṛ tih
anēkakōtibrahmāndajananī
divyavigrahā (124)

615 **Adishakthi**—She who is the primeval force.

616 **Ameya**—She who cannot be measured.

617 **Atma**—She who is the soul.

618 **Parama**—She who is better than all others.

619 **Pavana krithi**—She who is personification of purity.

620 **Aneka koti Bramanda janani**—She who is the mother of several billions of universes.

621 **Divya Vigraha**—She who is beautifully made.

क्लींकारी केवला गुह्या कैवल्य-पददायिनी ।
त्रिपुरा त्रिजगद्वन्द्या त्रिमूर्तिस्त्रिदशेश्वरी ।।१२५।।

klīṅkārīkēvalā guhyā
kaivalyapadadāyinī
tripurā trijagadvandyā
trimūrtih tridaśēśvarī (125)

622 **Klim karee**—She who is the shape of 'Klim'.

623 **Kevalaa**—She who is she herself.

624 **Guhya**—She who is secret.

625 **Kaivalya Padha dhayini**—She who gives redemption as well as position.

626 **Tripura**—She who lives everything in three aspects.

627 **Trijagat vandhya**—She who is worshipped by all in three worlds.

628 **Trimurthi**—She who is the trinity.

629 **Tri daseswari**—She who is the goddess for all gods.

त्र्यक्षरी दिव्य-गन्धाढ्या सिन्दूर-तिलकाञ्चिता ।
उमा शैलेन्द्रतनया गौरी गन्धर्व-सेविता ।।१२६।।

tryakṣarī divyagandhādhyā
sindūratilakāñcitā
umā śailēndratanayā gaurī
gandharvasēvitā (126)

630 **Tryakshya**—She who is of the form of three letters.

631 **Divya Gandhadya**—She who has godly smell.

632 **Sindhura thila kanchidha**—She who wears the sindhoora dot in her forehead

633 **Uma**—She who is in 'om'.

634 **Sailendra Thanaya**—She who is the daughter of the king of mountains.

635 **Gowri**—She who is white coloured.

636 **Gandharwa Sevitha**—She who is worshipped by gandharwas.

विश्वगर्भा स्वर्णगर्भाऽवरदा वागधीश्वरी ।
ध्यानगम्याऽपरिच्छेद्या ज्ञानदा ज्ञानविग्रहा ।।१२७।।

viśvagarbhā svarnagarbhā
varadā vāgadhīśvarī
dhyānagamyāyāparicchēdyā
jñānadā jñānavigrahā (127)

637 **Viswa Grabha**—She who carries the universe in her belly.

638 **Swarna Garbha**—She who is personification of gold.

639 **Avaradha**—She who punishes bad people

640 **Vagadeeswaree**—She who is the goddess of words.

641 **Dhyanagamya**—She who can be attained by meditation.

642 **Aparichedya**—She who cannot be predicted to be in a certain place.

643 **Gnadha**—She who gives out knowledge.

644 **Gnana Vigraha**—She who is personification of knowledge.

सर्ववेदान्त-संवेद्या सत्यानन्द-स्वरूपिणी ।
लोपामुद्रार्चिता लीला-कॢप्त-ब्रह्माण्ड-मण्डला ।।१२८।।

sarvavēdāntasaṁvēdyā
satyānandasvarūpinī
lōpāmudrārcitā līlāklipta
brahmāndamandalā (128)

645 **Sarva vedhantha samvedya**—She who can be known by all Upanishads.

646 **Satyananda swaroopini**—She who is personification of truth and happiness.

647 **Lopa mudrarchitha**—She who is worshipped by Lopa Mudhra the wife of Agasthya.

648 **Leela kluptha brahmanda mandala**—She who creates the different universes by simple play.

अदृश्या दृश्यरहिता विज्ञात्री वेद्यवर्जिता ।
योगिनी योगदा योग्या योगानन्दा युगन्धरा ।।१२९।।

adr̥ śyā dr̥ śyarahitā
vijñātrī vēdyavarjitā
yōginī yōgadāyōgyā
yōgānandā yugandharā (129)

649 **Adurshya**—She who cannot be seen.

650 **Drusya rahitha**—She who does not see things differently.

651 **Vignathree**—She who knows all sciences.

652 **Vedhya varjitha**—She who does not have any need to know anything.

653 **Yogini**—She who is personification of Yoga.

654 **Yogadha**—She who gives knowledge and experience of yoga.

655 **Yogya**—She who can be reached by yoga.

656 **Yogananda**—She who gets pleasure out of yoga.

657 **Yugandhara**—She who wears the yuga (Division of eons of time).

इच्छाशक्ति-ज्ञानशक्ति-क्रियाशक्ति-स्वरूपिणी ।
सर्वाधारा सुप्रतिष्ठा सदसद्रूप-धारिणी ।।१३०।।

icchāśaktijñānaśakti
kriyāśaktisvarūpinī
sarvādhārā supratiṣthā
sadasadrūpadhārinī (130)

658 **Iccha shakthi-Gnana shakthi-Kriya shakthi swaroopini**—'She who has desire as her head, Knowledge as her body and work as her feet'.

659 **Sarvaadhara**—She who is the basis of everything.

660 **Suprathishta**—She who is the best place of stay.

661 **Sada sadroopa dharini**—She who always has truth in her.

अष्टमूर्तिरजाजैत्री लोकयात्रा-विधायिनी ।
एकाकिनी भूमरूपा निर्द्वैता द्वैतवर्जिता ।।१३१।।

aṣṭamūrtirajājaitrī
lōkayātrāvidhāyinī
ēkākinī bhūmarūpā
nirdvaitā dvaitavarjitā (131)

662 **Ashta moorthy**—She who has eight forms.

663 **Aja jethree**—She who has won over ignorance.

664 **Loka yathra vidahyini**—She who makes the world rotate(travel).

665 **Ekakini**—She who is only herself and alone.

666 **Bhooma roopa**—She who is what we see, hear and understand.

667 **Nirdwaitha**—She who makes everything as one.

668 **Dwaitha varjitha**—She who is away from more than one.

अन्नदा वसुदा वृद्धा ब्रह्मात्मैक्य-स्वरूपिणी ।
बृहती ब्राह्मणी ब्राह्मी ब्रह्मानन्दा बलिप्रिया ।।१३२।।

annadā vasudā vr̥ ddhā
brahmātmaikyasvarūpinī
br̥ hatī brāhmanī brāhmī
brahmānandā balipriyā (132)

669 **Annadha**—She who gives food.
670 **Vasudha**—She who gives wealth.
671 **Vriddha**—She who is old.
672 **Brhmatmykya swaroopini**—She who merges herself in brahma-the ultimate truth.
673 **Brihathi**—She who is big.
674 **Brahmani**—She who is the wife of easwara.
675 **Brahmi**—She who has one aspect of Brhma.
676 **Brahmananda**—She who is the ultimate happiness.
677 **Bali priya**—She who likes the strong.

भाषारूपा बृहत्सेना भावाभाव-विवर्जिता ।
सुखाराध्या शुभकरी शोभना सुलभा गतिः ।।१३३।।

bhāṣārūpā br̥ hatsēnā
bhāvābhāvavivarjitā
sukhārādhyā śubhakarī
śōbhanā sulabhāgatīḥ (133)

678 **Bhasha roopa**—She who is personification of language.

679 **Brihat sena**—She who has big army.

680 **Bhavabhava vivarjitha**—She who does not have birth or death.

681 **Sukharadhya**—She who can be worshipped with pleasure.

682 **Shubhakaree**—She who does good.

683 **Shobhana sulabha gathi**—She who is easy to attain and does only good.

राज-राजेश्वरी राज्य-दायिनी राज्य-वल्लभा ।
राजत्कृपा राजपीठ-निवेशित-निजाश्रिता ।।१३४।।

rājarājēśvarī rājyadāyinī
rājyavallabhā
rājatkr̥ pā rājapītha
nivēśitanijāśritā (134)

684 **Raja rajeswari**—She who is goddess to king of kings like Devaraja, Yaksha raja, Brahma, Vishnu, and Rudra.

685 **Rajya Dhayini**—She who gives kingdoms like Vaikunta, Kailasa, etc.

686 **Rajya vallabha**—She who likes such kingdoms.

687 **Rajat krupa**—She whose mercy shines everywhere.

688 **Raja peetha nivesitha nijasritha**—She who makes people approaching her as kings.

राज्यलक्ष्मीः कोशनाथा चतुरङ्ग-बलेश्वरी ।
साम्राज्य-दायिनी सत्यसन्धा सागरमेखला ।।१३५।।

rājyalakṣmī kōśanāthā
caturaṁgabalēśvarī
sāmrājyadāyinī satyasandhā
sāgaramēkhalā (135)

689 **Rajya lakshmi**—She who is the wealth of kingdoms.

690 **Kosa natha**—She who protects the treasury.

691 **Chathuranga baleswai**—She who is the leader of the four fold army (Mind, brain, thought and ego).

692 **Samrajya Dhayini**—She who makes you emperor.

693 **Sathya Sandha**—She who is truthful.

694 **Sagara Mekhala**—She who is the earth surrounded by the sea.

दीक्षिता दैत्यशमनी सर्वलोक-वशङ्करी ।
सर्वार्थदात्री सावित्री सच्चिदानन्द-रूपिणी ।।१३६।।

dīkṣitā daityaśamanī
sarvalōkavaśaṅkarī
sarvārthadātrī sāvitrī
saccidānandarūpinī (136)

695 **Deekshitha**—She who gives the right to do fire sacrifice.

696 **Dhaitya Shamani**—She who controls anti gods.

697 **Sarva loka vasam kari**—She who keeps all the world within her control.

698 **Sarvartha Dhatri**—She who gives all wealth.

699 **Savithri**—She who is shines like the sun.

700 **Sachidananda roopini**—She who is personification of the ultimate truth.

देश-कालापरिच्छिन्ना सर्वगा सर्वमोहिनी ।
सरस्वती शास्त्रमयी गुहाम्बा गुह्यरूपिणी ।।१३७।।

dēśakālāparicchinnā
sarvagāsarvamōhinī
sarasvatī śāstramayī
guhāṁbā guhyarūpinī (137)

701 **Desa kala parischinna**—She who is not divided by region or time.

702 **Sarvaga**—She who is full of everywhere.

703 **Sarva mohini**—She who attracts every thing.

704 **Saraswathi**—She who is the goddess of knowledge.

705 **Sasthra mayi**—She who is the meaning of sciences.

706 **Guhamba**—She who is mother of Lord Subrahmanya (Guha).

707 **Guhya roopini**—She whose form is hidden from all.

सर्वोपाधि-विनिर्मुक्ता सदाशिव-पतिव्रता ।
सम्प्रदायेश्वरी साध्वी गुरुमण्डल-रूपिणी ।।१३८।।

sarvōpādhivinirmuktā
sadāśivapativratā
sampradāyēśvarī sādhvī
gurumandalarūpinī (138)

708 **Sarvo padhi vinirmuktha**—She who does not have any doctrines.

709 **Sada shiva pathi vritha**—She who is devoted wife for all times to Lord Shiva.

710 **Sampradhayeshwari**—She who is goddess to rituals or She who is goddess to teacher-student hierarchy.

711 **Sadhu**—She who is innocent.

712 **Ee**—She who is the letter 'e'.

713 **Guru mandala roopini**—She who is the universe round teachers.

कुलोत्तीर्णा भगाराध्या माया मधुमती मही ।
गणाम्बा गुह्यकाराध्या कोमलाङ्गी गुरुप्रिया ।।१३६।।

kulōttīrṇā bhagārādhyā
māyā madhumatī mahī
ganāṁbā guhyakārādhyā
kōmalāṁgī gurupriyā (139)

714 **Kulotheerna**—She who is beyond the group of senses.

715 **Bhagaradhya**—She who is to be worshipped in the universe round the sun.

716 **Maya**—She who is illusion.

717 **Madhumathi**—She who is the trance stage (seventh) in yoga.

718 **Mahee**—She who is personification of earth.

719 **Ganamba**—She who is mother to Ganesha and bhootha ganas.

720 **Guhyakaradhya**—She who should be worshipped in secret places.

721 **Komalangi**—She who has beautiful limbs.

722 **Guru Priya**—She who likes teachers.

स्वतन्त्रा सर्वतन्त्रेशी दक्षिणामूर्ति-रूपिणी ।
सनकादि-समाराध्या शिवज्ञान-प्रदायिनी ।।१४०।।

svatantrā sarvatantrēśī
dakṣināmūrtirūpinī
sanakādi samārādhyā
śivajñānapradāyinī (140)

723 **Swathanthra**—She who is independent.

724 **Sarwa thanthresi**—She who is goddess to all thanthras (tricks to attain God).

725 **Dakshina moorthi roopini**—She who is the personification of God facing South (The teacher form of Shiva).

726 **Sanakadhi samaradhya**—She who is being worshipped by Sanaka sages.

727 **Siva gnana pradhayini**—She who gives the knowledge of God.

चित्कलाऽऽनन्द-कलिका प्रेमरूपा प्रियङ्करी ।
नामपारायण-प्रीता नन्दिविद्या नटेश्वरी ।।१४१।।

citkalānandakalikā
prēmarūpā priyaṅkarī
nāmapārāyanaprītā
nandividyānatēśvarī (141)

728 **Chid kala**—She who is the micro power deep within.

729 **Ananda Kalika**—She who is the happiness in beings.

730 **Prema roopa**—She who is the form of love.

731 **Priyamkaree**—She who does what is liked.

732 **Nama parayana preetha**—She who likes repetition of her various names.

733 **Nandhi vidhya**—She who is the knowledge taught by Nandi deva (The bull god on whom shiva rides).

734 Nateshwaree—She who is the goddess of dance.

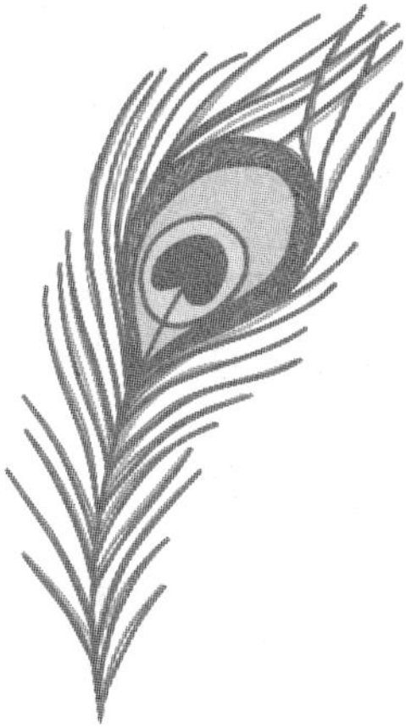

मिथ्या-जगदधिष्ठाना मुक्तिदा मुक्तिरूपिणी ।
लास्यप्रिया लयकरी लज्जा रम्भादिवन्दिता ।।१४२।।

mithyājagadadhiṣṭhānā
muktidā muktirūpinī
lāsyapriyā layakarī
lajjā raṁbhādivanditā (142)

735 **Mithya Jagat athishtana**—She who is luck to this world of illusion.

736 **Mukthida**—She who gives redemption.

737 **Mukthiroopini**—She who is redemption.

738 **Lasya priya**—She who likes feminine dance.

739 **Laya karee**—She who is the bridge between dance and music.

740 **Lajja**—She who is shy.

741 **Rambha adhi vandhitha**—She who is worshipped by the celestial dancers.

भवदाव-सुधावृष्टिः पापारण्य-दवानला ।
दौर्भाग्य-तूलवातूला जराध्वान्त-रविप्रभा ।।१४३।।

bhavadāvasudhāvr̥ ṣṭih
pāpāranyadavānalā
daurbhāgyatūlavātūlā
jarādhvāntaraviprabhā (143)

742 **Bhava dhava sudha vrishti**—She who douses the forest fire of the sad life of mortals with a rain of nectar.

743 **Paparanya dhavanala**—She who is the forest fire that destroys the forest of sin.

744 **Daurbhagya thoolavathoola**—She who is the cyclone that blows away the cotton of bad luck.

745 **Jaradwanthara viprabha**—She who is the suns rays that swallows the darkness of old age.

भाग्याब्धि-चन्द्रिका भक्त-चित्तकेकि-घनाघना ।
रोगपर्वत-दम्भोर्लि मृत्युदारु-कुठारिका ।।१४४।।

bhāgyābdhicandrikā
bhaktacittakēkīghanāghanā
rōgaparvatadaṁbhōlir
mr̥ tyudārukuthārikā (144)

746 **Bhagyabdhi chandrika**—She who is the full moon to the sea of luck.

747 **Bhaktha Chitta Keki Ganagana**—She who is the black cloud to the peacock which is he devotees mind.

748 **Roga parvatha Dhambola**—She who is the Vajra weapon which breaks the sickness which is like the mountain.

749 **Mrutyu Dharu Kudarika**—She who is like the axe which fells the tree of death.

महेश्वरी महाकाली महाग्रासा महाशना ।
अपर्णा चण्डिका चण्डमुण्डासुर-निषूदिनी ।।१४५।।

mahēśvarī mahākālī
mahāgrāsā mahāśanā
aparnā candikā
candamundāsuraniṣūdinī (145)

750 **Maheswaree**—She who is the greatest goddess.

751 **Maha kali**—She who is the great Kalee.

752 **Maha grasa**—She who is like a great drinking bowl.

753 **Mahasana**—She who is the great eater.

754 **Aparna**—She who did meditation without even eating a leaf.

755 **Chandika**—She who is supremely angry

756 **Chanda mundasura nishoodhini**—She who killed the asuras called Chanda and Munda.

क्षराक्षरात्मिका सर्व-लोकेशी विश्वधारिणी ।
त्रिवर्गदात्री सुभगा त्र्यम्बका त्रिगुणात्मिका ।।१४६।।

kṣarākṣarātmikā
sarvalōkēśī viśvadhārinī
trivargadātrī subhagā
tryaṁbakā trigunātmikā (146)

757 **Ksharaksharathmika**—She who can never be destroyed and also destroyed.

758 **Sarva lokesi**—She who is goddess to all the worlds.

759 **Viswa Dharini**—She who carries all the universe.

760 **Thrivarga Dhathri**—She who gives dharma, Assets and pleasure.

761 **Subhaga**—She who is pleasing to look at.

762 **Thryambhaga**—She who has three eyes.

763 **Trigunathmika**—She who is personification of three gunas viz., Thamo (Kali), Rajo (Dhurga), and Sathva (Parvathy).

स्वर्गापवर्गदा शुद्धा जपापुष्प-निभाकृतिः ।
ओजोवती द्युतिधरा यज्ञरूपा प्रियव्रता ।।१४७।।

svargāpavargadā śuddhā
japāpuṣpanibhākr̥ tih
ōjōvatī dyutidharā
yajñarūpā priyavratā (147)

764 **Swargapavargadha**—She who gives heaven and the way to it.

765 **Shuddha**—She who is clean.

766 **Japapushpa nibhakrithi**—She who has the colour of hibiscus.

767 **Ojovathi**—She who is full of vigour.

768 **Dhyuthidhara**—She who has light.

769 **Yagna roopa**—She who is of the form of sacrifice.

770 **Priyavrudha**—She who likes penances.

दुराराध्या दुराधर्षा पाटली-कुसुम-प्रिया ।
महती मेरुनिलया मन्दार-कुसुम-प्रिया ।।१४८।।

durārādhyā durādharṣā
pātalīkusumapriyā
mahatī mērunilayā
mandārakusumapriyā (148)

771 **Dhuraradhya**—She who is rarely available for worship.

772 **Dhuradharsha**—She who cannot be won.

773 **Patali kusuma priya**—She who likes the buds of Patali tree.

774 **Mahathi**—She who is big.

775 **Meru nilaya**—She who lives in Meru mountain.

776 **Mandhara kusuma priya**—She who likes the buds of Mandhara tree.

वीराराध्या विराड्रूपा विरजा विश्वतोमुखी ।
प्रत्यग्रूपा पराकाशा प्राणदा प्राणरूपिणी ।।१४६।।

vīrārādhyā virādrūpā
virajā viśvatōmukhī
pratyagrūpā parākāśā
prānadā prānarūpinī (149)

777 **Veeraradhya**—She who is worshipped by heroes.

778 **Virad Roopa**—She who a universal look.

779 **Viraja**—She who does not have any blemish.

780 **Viswathomukhi**—She who sees through every ones eyes.

781 **Prathyg roopa**—She who can be seen by looking inside.

782 **Parakasa**—She who is the great sky.

783 **Pranadha**—She who gives the soul.

मार्ताण्ड-भैरवाराध्या मन्त्रिणीन्यस्त-राज्यधूः ।
त्रिपुरेशी जयत्सेना निस्त्रैगुण्या परापरा ॥१५०॥

mārtāndabhairavārādhyā
mantrinīnyastarājyadhūh
tripurēśī jayatsēnā
nistraiguṇyā parāparā (150)

784 **Prana roopini**—She who is the soul.

785 **Marthanda Bhairavaradhya**—She who is being worshipped by Marthanda Bhairava.

786 **Manthrini nyashtha rajyadhoo**—She who gave the power to rule to her form of Manthrini.

787 **Tripuresi**—She who is the head of three cities.

788 **Jayatsena**—She who has an army which wins.

789 **Nistrai gunya**—She who is above the three qualities.

790 **Parapara**—She who is outside and inside.

सत्य-ज्ञानानन्द-रूपा सामरस्य-परायणा ।
कपर्दिनी कलामाला कामधुक्कामरूपिणी ।।१५१।।

satyajñānānandarūpā
sāmarasyaparāyanā
kapardinī kalāmālā
kāmadhuk kāmarūpinī (151)

791 **Satya gnananda roopa**—She who is personification of truth, knowledge and happiness.

792 **Samarasya parayana**—She who stands in peace.

793 **Kapardhini**—She who is the wife of Kapardhi (Siva with hair).

794 **Kalamala**—She who wears arts as garlands.

795 **Kamadhukh**—She who fulfills desires.

796 **Kama roopini**—She who can take any form.

कलानिधिः काव्यकला रसज्ञा रसशेवधिः ।
पुष्टा पुरातना पूज्या पुष्करा पुष्करेक्षणा ।।१५२।।

kalānidhih kāvyakalā
rasajñā rasaśēvadhīh
puṣtā purātanā pūjyā
puṣkarā puṣkarēkṣanā (152)

797 **Kala nidhi**—She who is the treasure of arts.

798 **Kavya kala**—She who is the art of writing.

799 **Rasagna**—She who appreciates arts.

800 **Rasa sevadhi**—She who is the treasure of arts.

801 **Pushta**—She who is healthy.

802 **Purathana**—She who is ancient.

803 **Poojya**—She who is fit to be worshipped.

804 **Pushkara**—She who gives exuberance.

805 **Pushkarekshana**—She who has lotus like eyes.

परंज्योतिः परंधाम परमाणुः परात्परा ।
पाशहस्ता पाशहन्त्री परमन्त्र-विभेदिनी ।।१५३।।

paraṁjyōtih paraṁdhāma
paramānuh parātparā
pāśahastā pāśahantrī
paramantravibhēdinī (153)

806 **Paramjyothi**—She who is the ultimate light.

807 **Param dhama**—She who is the ultimate resting place.

808 **Paramanu**—She who is the ultimate atom.

809 **Parath para**—She who is better than the best.

810 **Pasa Hastha**—She who has rope in her hand.

811 **Pasa Hanthri**—She who cuts off attachment.

812 **Para manthra Vibhedini**—She who destroys the effect of spells cast.

मूर्ताऽमूर्ताऽनित्यतृप्ता मुनिमानस-हंसिका ।
सत्यव्रता सत्यरूपा सर्वान्तर्यामिनी सती ।।१५४।।

mūrtāmūrtā nityatṛ ptā
munimānasahaṁsikā
satyavratā satyarūpā
sarvāntaryāminī satī (154)

813 **Moortha**—She who has a form.

814 **Amoortha**—She who does not have a form.

815 **Anithya thriptha**—She who gets happy with prayers using temporary things.

816 **Muni manasa hamsika**—She who is the swan in the mind (lake like) of sages.

817 **Satya vritha**—She who has resolved to speak only truth.

818 **Sathya roopa**—She who is the real form.

819 **Sarvantharyamini**—She who is within everything.

820 **Sathee**—She who is Sathee the daughter of Daksha.

ब्रह्माणी ब्रह्मजननी बहुरूपा बुधार्चिता ।
प्रसवित्री प्रचण्डाऽऽज्ञा प्रतिष्ठा प्रकटाकृतिः ।।१५५।।

brahmānī brahmajananī
bahurūpā budhārcitā
prasavitrī pracandājñā
pratiṣthā prakatākṛ tih (155)

821 **Brahmani**—She who is the strength behind creator.
822 **Brahmaa**—She who is the creator.
823 **Janani**—She who is the mother.
824 **Bahu roopa**—She who has several forms.
825 **Budharchitha**—She who is being worshipped by the enlightened.
826 **Prasavithri**—She who has given birth to everything.
827 **Prachanda**—She who is very angry.
828 **Aagna**—She who is the order.
829 **Prathishta**—She who has been installed.
830 **Prakata Krithi**—She who is clearly visible.

श्री

प्राणेश्वरी प्राणदात्री पञ्चाशत्पीठ-रूपिणी ।
विशृङ्खला विविक्तस्था वीरमाता वियत्प्रसूः ।।१५६।।

prāṇēśvarī prāṇadātrī
pañcāśatpīṭharūpiṇī
viśṛ ṁkhalā viviktasthā
vīramātā viyatprasūḥ (156)

831 Praneshwari—She who is goddess to the soul.

832 Prana Dhatri—She who gives the soul.

833 Panchast peeta roopini—She who is in the form of fifty Shakti Peethas.

834 Vishungala—She who is not chained.

835 Vivikthastha—She who is in lonely places.

836 Veera matha—She who is the mother of heroes.

837 Viyat prasoo—She who has created the sky.

मुकुन्दा मुक्तिनिलया मूलविग्रह-रूपिणी ।
भावज्ञा भवरोगघ्नी भवचक्र-प्रवर्तिनी ।।१५७।।

mukundā muktinilayā
mūlavigraharūpinī
bhāvajñā bhavarōgaghnī
bhavacakrapravartinī (157)

838 **Mukundaa**—She who gives redemption.

839 **Mukthi nilaya**—She who is the seat of redemption.

840 **Moola vigraha roopini**—She who is the basic statue.

841 **Bavagna**—She who understands wishes and thoughts.

842 **Bhava rokagni**—She who cures the sin of birth.

843 **Bhava Chakra Pravarthani**—She makes the wheel of birth rotate.

छन्दःसारा शास्त्रसारा मन्त्रसारा तलोदरी ।
उदारकीर्तिरुद्दामवैभवा वर्णरूपिणी ।।१५८।।

chandahsārā śāstrasārā
mantrasārā talōdarī
udārakīrtīruddāmavaibhavā
varnarūpinī (158)

844 **Chanda sara**—She who is the meaning of Vedas.

845 **Sasthra sara**—She who is the meaning of Puranas (epics).

846 **Manthra sara**—She who is the meaning of Manthras (chants).

847 **Thalodharee**—She who has a small belly.

848 **Udara keerthi**—She who has wide and tall fame.

849 **Uddhhama vaibhava**—She who has immeasurable fame.

850 **Varna roopini**—She who is personification of alphabets.

जन्ममृत्यु-जरातप्त-जनविश्रान्ति-दायिनी ।
सर्वोपनिषद्-दुद्-घुष्टा शान्त्यतीत-कलात्मिका ।।१५६।।

janmamr̥ tyujarātapta
janaviśrāntidāyinī
sarvōpaniṣadudghuṣṭā
śāntyatītakalātmikā (159)

851 **Janma mrutyu jara thaptha jana vishranthi dhayini**—She who is the panacea of ills of birth, death, and aging.

852 **Sarvopanisha dhudh gushta**—She who is being loudly announced as the greatest by Upanishads.

853 **Shantyathheetha kalathmika**—She who is a greater art than peace.

गम्भीरा गगनान्तस्था गर्विता गानलोलुपा ।
कल्पना-रहिता काष्ठाऽकान्ता कान्तार्ध-विग्रहा ॥१६०॥

gaṁbhīrā gaganāntasthā
garvitā gānalōlupā
kalpanārahitā kāṣṭhā kāntā
kāntārdhavigrahā (160)

854 **Gambheera**—She whose depth cannot be measured.

855 **Gagananthastha**—She who is situated in the sky.

856 **Garvitha**—She who is proud.

857 **Gana lolupa**—She who likes songs.

858 **Kalpana rahitha**—She who does not imagine.

859 **Kashta**—She who is in the ultimate boundary.

860 **Akantha**—She who removes sins.

861 **Kanthatha vigraha**—She who is half of her husband (kantha).

कार्यकारण-निर्मुक्ता कामकेलि-तरङ्गिता ।
कनत्कनकता-टङ्का लीला-विग्रह-धारिणी ।।१६१।।

kāryakāraṇanirmuktā
kāmakēlitaraṁgitā
kanatkanakatāṭaṅkā
līlāvigrahadhāriṇī (161)

862 **Karya karana nirmuktha**—She who is beyond the action and the cause.

863 **Kama keli tharangitha**—She who is the waves of the sea of the play of the God.

864 **Kanath kanaka thadanga**—She who wears the glittering golden ear studs.

865 **Leela vigraha dharini**—She who assumes several forms as play.

अजा क्षयविनिर्मुक्ता मुग्धा क्षिप्र-प्रसादिनी ।
अन्तर्मुख-समाराध्या बहिर्मुख-सुदुर्लभा ।।१६२।।

ajākṣayavinirmuktā
mugdhā kṣipraprasādinī
antarmukhasamārādhyā
bahirmukhasudurlabhā (162)

866 **Ajha**—She who does not have birth.

867 **Kshaya nirmuktha**—She who does not have death.

868 **Gubdha**—She who is beautiful.

869 **Ksipra prasadhini**—She who is pleased quickly.

870 **Anthar mukha samaradhya**—She who is worshipped by internal thoughts.

871 **Bahir mukha sudurlabha**—She who can be attained by external prayers.

त्रयी त्रिवर्गनिलया त्रिस्था त्रिपुरमालिनी ।
निरामया निरालम्बा स्वात्मारामा सुधासृतिः ।।१६३।।

trayī trivarganilayā
tristhā tripuramālinī
nirāmayā nirālaṁbā
svātmārāmā sudhāsr̥ tih (163)

872 **Thrayee**—She who is of the form of three Vedas viz. RIg, Yajur, and Sama.

873 **Trivarga nilaya**—She who is in three aspects of self, assets and pleasure.

874 **Thristha**—She who is in three.

875 **Tripura malini**—She who is in tripura the sixth section of Srichakra.

876 **Niramaya**—She who is without diseases.

877 **Niralamba**—She who does not need another birth.

878 **Swatma rama**—She who enjoys within herself.

879 **Sudha sruthi**—She who is the rain of nectar.

संसारपङ्क-निर्मग्न-समुद्धरण-पण्डिता ।
यज्ञप्रिया यज्ञकर्त्री यजमान-स्वरूपिणी ।।१६४।।

samsārapankanirmagna
samuddharanapanditā
yajñapriyā yajñakartrī
yajamānasvarūpinī (164)

880 **Samsara panga nirmagna samuddharana panditha**—She who is capable of saving people who drown in the mud of day today life.

881 **Yagna priya**—She who likes fire sacrifice

882 **Yagna karthree**—She who carries out fire sacrifice.

883 **Yajamana swaroopini**—She who is the doer of fire sacrifice.

धर्माधारा धनाध्यक्षा धनधान्य-विवर्धिनी ।
विप्रप्रिया विप्ररूपा विश्वभ्रमण-कारिणी ।।१६५।।

dharmādhārā dhanādhyakṣā
dhanadhānyavivardhinī
viprapriyā viprarūpā
viśvabhramanakārinī (165)

884 **Dharma dhara**—She who is the basis of Dharma-the rightful action.

885 **Dhanadyaksha**—She who presides over wealth.

886 **Dhanadhanya vivardhani**—She who makes wealth and grain to grow.

887 **Vipra priya**—She who likes those who learn Vedas.

888 **Vipra roopa**—She who is the learner of Vedas.

889 **Viswa brhamana karini**—She who makes the universe to rotate.

विश्वग्रासा विद्रुमाभा वैष्णवी विष्णुरूपिणी ।
अयोनिर्योनिनिलया कूटस्था कुलरूपिणी ।।१६६।।

viśvagrāsā vidrumābhā
vaiṣnavī viṣnurūpinī
ayōnir- yōninilayā
kūtasthā kularūpinī (166)

890 **Viswa grasa**—She who eats the universe in one handful.

891 **Vidhrumabha**—She who has the luster of coral.

892 **Vaishnavi**—She who is the power of Vishnu.

893 **Vishnu roopini**—She who is Vishnu.

894 **Ayoni**—She who does not have a cause or She who is not born.

895 **Yoni nilaya**—She who is the cause and source of everything.

896 **Kootastha**—She who is stable.

897 **Kula roopini**—She who is personification of culture.

वीरगोष्ठीप्रिया वीरा नैष्कर्म्या नादरूपिणी ।
विज्ञानकलना कल्या विदग्धा बैन्दवासना ।।१६७।।

vīragōṣthipriyā vīrā
naiṣkarmyā nādarūpinī
vijñānakalanā kalyā
vidagddhā baindavāsanā (167)

898 **Veera goshti priya**—She who likes company of heroes.

899 **Veera**—She who has valour.

900 **Naish karmya**—She who does not have attachment to action.

901 **Nadha roopini**—She who is the form of sound.

902 **Vignana kalana**—She who makes science.

903 **Kalya**—She who is expert in arts.

904 **Vidhagdha**—She who is an expert.

905 **Baindavasana**—She who sits in the dot of the thousand petalled lotus.

श्री

तत्त्वाधिका तत्त्वमयी तत्त्वमर्थ-स्वरूपिणी ।
सामगानप्रिया सौम्या सदाशिव-कुटुम्बिनी ।।१६८।।

tattvādhikā tattvamayī
tattvamarthasvarūpinī
sāmagānapriyā sōmyā
sadāśivakutumbinī (168)

906 **Tathwadhika**—She who is above all metaphysics.

907 **Tatwa mayee**—She who is Metaphysics.

908 **Tatwa Martha swaroopini**—She who is personification of this and that.

909 **Sama gana priya**—She who likes singing of sama.

910 **Soumya**—She who is peaceful or She who is as pretty as the moon.

911 **Sada shiva kutumbini**—She who is consort of Sada shiva.

सव्यापसव्य-मार्गस्था सर्वापद्विनिवारिणी ।
स्वस्था स्वभावमधुरा धीरा धीरसमर्चिता ।।१६६।।

savyāpasavyamārgasthā
sarvāpadvinivārinī
svasthā svabhāvamadhurā
dhīrā dhīrasamarcitā (169)

912 **Savyapa savya margastha**—She who is birth, death and living or She who likes the priestly and tantric methods.

913 **Sarva apadvi nivarini**—She who removes all dangers.

914 **Swastha**—She who has everything within her or She who is peaceful.

915 **Swabhava madura**—She who is by nature sweet.

916 **Dheera**—She who is courageous.

917 **Dheera samarchida**—She who is being worshipped by the courageous.

चौतन्यार्घ्य-समाराध्या चैतन्य-कुसुमप्रिया ।
सदोदिता सदातुष्टा तरुणादित्य-पाटला ।।१७०।।

caitanyār-ghyasamārādhyā
caitanyakusumapriyā
sadōditā sadātuṣṭā
tarunādityapātalā (170)

918 **Chaithnyarkya samaradhya**—She who is worshipped by the ablation of water.

919 **Chaitanya kusuma priya**—She who likes the never fading flowers.

920 **Saddothitha**—She who never sets.

921 **Sadha thushta**—She who is always happy.

922 **Tharunadithya patala**—She who like the young son is red mixed with white.

दक्षिणा-दक्षिणाराध्या दरस्मेर-मुखाम्बुजा ।
कौलिनी-केवलाऽनर्घ्य-कैवल्य-पददायिनी ।।१७१।।

dakṣiṇādakṣiṇārādhyā
darasmēramukhāṁbujā
kaulinī kēvalānar
ghyakaivalyapadadāyinī (171)

923 **Dakshina Daksinaradhya**—She who is worshipped by the learned and ignorant.

924 **Dharasmera mukhambuja**—She who has a smiling face like the lotus in full bloom.

925 **Kaulini kevala**—She who is mixture of the koula and kevala methods.

926 **Anargya kaivalya pada dhayini**—She who gives the immeasurable heavenly stature.

श्री

स्तोत्रप्रिया स्तुतिमती श्रुति-संस्तुत-वैभवा ।
मनस्विनी मानवती महेशी मङ्गलाकृतिः ।।१७२।।

stōtrapriyā stutimatī
śrutisaṁstutavaibhavā
manasvinī mānavatī
mahēśī maṁgalākṛ tih (172)

927 **Stotra priya**—She who likes chants.

928 **Sthuthi mathi**—She who gives boons for those who sing her chants.

929 **Sthuthi samsthutha vaibhava**—She who is worshipped by the Vedas.

930 **Manaswaini**—She who has a stable mind.

931 **Manavathi**—She who has big heart.

932 **Mahesi**—She who is the greatest goddess.

933 **Mangala kruthi**—She who does only good.

विश्वमाता जगद्धात्री विशालाक्षी विरागिणी ।
प्रगल्भा परमोदारा परामोदा मनोमयी ।।१७३।।

viśvamātā jagaddhātrī
viśālākṣī virāgini
pragadbhā paramōdārā
parāmōdā manōmayī (173)

934 **Viswa Matha**—The mother of the universe.

935 **Jagat Dhathri**—She who supports the world.

936 **Visalakshi**—She who is broad eyed.

937 **Viragini**—She who has renounced.

938 **Pragalbha**—She who is courageous.

939 **Paramodhara**—She who is great giver.

940 **Paramodha**—She who has great happiness.

941 **Manomayi**—She who is one with mind.

व्योमकेशी विमानस्था वज्रिणी वामकेश्वरी ।
पञ्चयज्ञ-प्रिया पञ्च-प्रेत-मञ्चाधिशायिनी ।।१७४।।

vyōmakēśī vimānasthā
vajrinī vāmakēśvarī
pañcayajñapriyā
pañcaprētamañcādhiśāyinī (174)

942 **Vyoma kesi**—She who is the wife of Shiva who has sky as his hair.

943 **Vimanastha**—She who is at the top.

944 **Vajrini**—She who has indra's wife as a part.

945 **Vamakeshwaree**—She who is goddess of the people who follow the left path.

946 **Pancha yagna priya**—She who likes the five sacrifices.

947 **Pancha pretha manchadhi sayini**—She who sleeps on the cot made of five corpses.

पञ्चमी पञ्चभूतेशी पञ्च-संख्योपचारिणी ।
शाश्वती शाश्वतैश्वर्या शर्मदा शम्भुमोहिनी ।।१७५।।

pañcamī pañcabhūtēśī
pañcasaṁkhyōpacāriṇī
śāśvatī śāśvadaiśvaryā
śarmadā śaṁbhumōhinī (175)

948 **Panchami**—She who is the consort of Sadshiva –the fifth of the pancha brahmas.

949 **Pancha bhoothesi**—"She who is the chief of Pancha bhoothas viz earth, sky, fire, air. And water".

950 **Pancha sankhyopacharini**—She who is worshipped by five offerings: sandalwood (Gandha), flowers (Pushpa), incense (Dhoopa), light (Dheepa), and food offerings (Naivedya).

951 **Saswathi**—She who is permanent.

952 **Saswathaiswarya**—She who gives perennial wealth.

953 **Sarmadha**—She who gives pleasure.

954 **Sambhu mohini**—She who bewitches Lord Shiva.

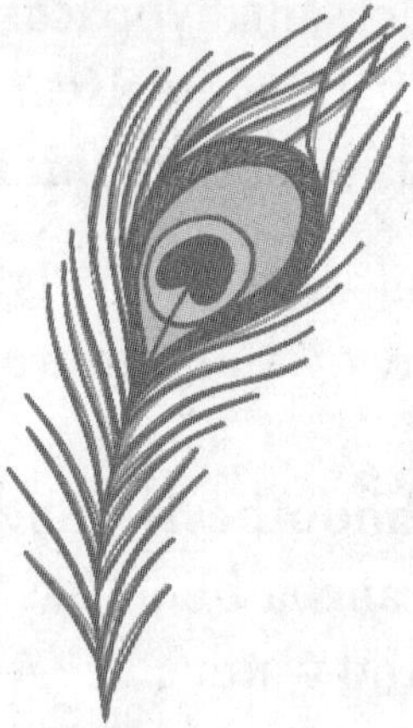

श्री

धरा धरसुता धन्या धर्मिणी धर्मवर्धिनी ।
लोकातीता गुणातीता सर्वातीता शमात्मिका ।।१७६।।

dharādharasutā dhanyā
dharminī dharmavardhinī
lōkātītā gunātītā
sarvātītā śamātmikā (176)

955 **Dhara**—She who carries (beings like earth).

956 **Dharasutha**—She who is the daughter of the mountain.

957 **Dhanya**—She who has all sort of wealth

958 **Dharmini**—She who likes dharma.

959 **Dharma vardhini**—She who makes dharma grow.

960 **Loka theetha**—She who is beyond the world.

961 **Guna theetha**—She who is beyond properties.

962 **Sarvatheetha**—She who is beyond everything.

963 **Samathmika**—She who is peace.

बन्धूक-कुसुमप्रख्या बाला लीलाविनोदिनी ।
सुमङ्गली सुखकरी सुवेषाढ्या सुवासिनी ।।१७७।।

bandhūkakusumaprakhyā
bālālīlāvinōdinī
sumamgalī sukhakarī
suvēṣādhyā suvāsinī (177)

964 **Bhandhooka kusuma prakhya**—She who has the glitter of bhandhooka flowers.

965 **Bala**—She who is a young maiden.

966 **Leela Vinodhini**—She who loves to play.

967 **Sumangali**—She who gives all good things.

968 **Sukha kari**—She who gives pleasure.

969 **Suveshadya**—She who is well made up.

970 **Suvasini**—She who is sweet scented (married woman).

सुवासिन्यर्चन-प्रीताऽऽशोभना शुद्धमानसा ।
बिन्दु-तर्पण-सन्तुष्टा पूर्वजा त्रिपुराम्बिका ।।१७८।।

suvāsinyarcanaprītāśōbhanā
śuddhamānasā
bindutarpanasantuṣṭā
pūrvajā tripurāṁbikā (178)

971 **Suvasinyarchana preetha**—She who likes the worship of married woman.

972 **Ashobhana**—She who has full glitter.

973 **Shuddha manasa**—She who has a clean mind.

974 **Bindhu tharpana santhushta**—She who is happy with the offering in the dot of Ananda maya chakra.

975 **Poorvaja**—She who preceded every one.

976 **Tripurambika**—She who is the goddess of three cities.

दशमुद्रा-समाराध्या त्रिपुराश्री-वशङ्करी ।
ज्ञानमुद्रा ज्ञानगम्या ज्ञानज्ञेय-स्वरूपिणी ।।१७६।।

daśamudrāsamārādhyā
tripurāśrīvaśaṅkarī
jñānamudrā jñānagamyā
jñānajñēyasvarūpinī (179)

977 **Dasa mudhra samaradhya**—She who is worshipped by ten mudras (postures of the hand).

978 **Thrpura sree vasankari**—She who keeps the goddess Tripura sree.

979 **Gnana mudhra**—She who shows the symbol of knowledge.

980 **Gnana gamya**—She who can be attained by knowledge.

981 **Gnana gneya swaroopini**—She who is what is thought and the thought.

योनिमुद्रा त्रिखण्डेशी त्रिगुणाम्बा त्रिकोणगा ।
अनघाऽद्भुत-चारित्रा वाञ्छितार्थ-प्रदायिनी ।।१८०।।

yōnimudrā trikhandēśī
trigunāṁbā trikōnagā
anaghādbhutacāritrā
vāñchitārthapradāyinī (180)

982 **Yoni mudhra**—She who shows the symbol of pleasure.

983 **Trikhandesi**—She who is the lord of three zones of fire, moon, and sun.

984 **Triguna**—She who is three characters.

985 **Amba**—She who is the mother.

986 **Trikonaga**—She who has attained at all vertices of a triangle.

987 **Anaga**—She who is not neared by sin.

988 **Adbutha charithra**—She who has a wonderful history.

989 **Vanchithartha pradayini**—She who gives what is desired.

अभ्यासातिशय-ज्ञाता षडध्वातीत-रूपिणी ।
अव्याज-करुणा-मूर्तिरज्ञान-ध्वान्त-दीपिका ।।१८१।।

abhyāsātiśayajñātā
ṣadaddhvātītarūpinī
avyājakarunāmūrtih
ajñānaddhvāntadīpikā (181)

990 **Abhyasathisaya gnatha**—She who can be realized by constant practice.

991 **Shaddwatheetha roopini**—She who supersedes the six methods of prayers.

992 **Avyaja karuna moorhy**—She who shows mercy without reason.

993 **Agnana dwantha deepika**—She who is the lamp that drives away ignorance.

आबाल-गोप-विदिता सर्वानुल्लङ्घय-शासना ।
श्रीचक्रराज-निलया श्रीमत्-त्रिपुरसुन्दरी ।।१८२।।

ābālagōpaviditā
sarvānullaṁghyaśāsanā
śrīcakrarājanilayā
śrīmattripurasundarī (182)

994 **Abala gopa vidhitha**—She who is worshipped by all right from children and cowherds.

995 **Sarvan ullangya sasana**—She whose orders can never be disobeyed.

996 **Sri chakra raja nilaya**—She who lives in Srichakra.

997 **Sri math thripura sundari**—The beautiful goddess of wealth who is consort of the Lord of Tripura.

श्रीशिवा शिव-शक्त्यैक्य-रूपिणी ललिताम्बिका ।
एवं श्रीललिता देव्या नाम्नां साहस्त्रकं जगुः ।।१८३।।

śrīśivā śivaśaktyaikyarūpinī
lalitāṁbikā
evaṃ śrīlalitā devyā
nāmnāṃ sāhasrakaṃ jaguḥ (183)

998 **Sri shivaa**—She who is the eternal peace.

999 **Shiva shakthaikya roopini**—She who is unification of Shiva and Shakthi.

1000 **Lalithambika**—The easily approachable mother.

।। इति श्रीब्रह्माण्डपुराणे उत्तरखण्डे
श्रीहयग्रीवागस्त्यसंवादे
श्रीललिता सहस्रनाम स्तोत्र कथनं सम्पूर्णम् ।।

iti śrībrahmāṇḍapurāṇe uttarakhaṇḍe
śrīhayagrīvāgastyasaṃvāde
śrīlalitā sahasranāma stotra
kathanaṃ sampūrṇam